THE PEPPERIDGE FARM BAKING BOOK

THE
PEPPERIDGE FARM
BAKING BOOK
By Margaret Rudkin

(CONTENTS SPECIALLY SELECTED FROM *The Margaret Rudkin Pepperidge Farm Cookbook*)

Illustrations by Erik Blegvad

GROSSET & DUNLAP, INC.
A National General Company

CONTENTS

Childhood   1

Country Life   17

Pepperidge Farm   25

Recipes   41

THE
PEPPERIDGE FARM
BAKING BOOK

CHILDHOOD

WHEN I was a child, I lived in a brownstone private house on a quiet street, paved with cobblestones, in the section of New York now known as Tudor City, high above the present United Nations Plaza.

The old narrow house was four stories high, with a stoop —an outside stairway of stone steps—leading up to the big front door. That word *stoop* is left over from the early Dutch settlement in New York and originally meant a platform with steps at the door of a house.

The wide stone steps were used by children for playing games, and on hot summer evenings we were allowed to sit there until dark, cooling off by eating enormous ice-cream cones, which cost five cents. If we didn't have a nickel, we sucked on a piece of ice dipped in sugar. We waited for the lamplighter to come by with his long lighting stick and, with a quick touch of the flaming tip, light up the gas mantle on the lamppost at the corner.

Sometimes at dusk the gypsies came, too, in the summertime, to tell our fortunes, mend the pots and pans and scamper off with anything lying around loose.

Years later a part of old New York disappeared when all those private houses were torn down to make way for big apartment buildings. All the houses in the block were exactly alike. At the front of each basement was the dining room, with the kitchen behind it, opening onto a small yard. Upstairs on the parlor floor, where you entered from the big door at the top of the stoop, were the "front parlor" best room and the "back parlor" everyday room. The bedrooms were on the third and fourth floors.

But the large, brick-floored kitchen was really the heart of the house. There was an enormous coal stove set back into the chimney wall, with a six-foot hearthstone in front of it. The gray stone laundry tubs stood along the opposite wall, and on laundry days not much cooking was done because the copper clothes boiler was steaming on the stove all day, with the laundress trotting back and forth from the tubs to the boiler, fishing the boiled laundry out of the bubbling water with a long "clothes stick" which had become soft and soggy from the constant hot-water dips. Woe betide anyone who got in her way!

I always wanted to eat lunch in the kitchen on laundry day, for it was sure to be cold boiled ham, soft, floury boiled potatoes and a mug of milk. I ate very slowly because I loved to sniff the spicy, soapy, steamy air, which I was told "cleared out your tubes." More important, the steam made my red hair curly, and I thought that improved my looks.

Our cooking was always simple and delicious—no fancy stuff and sauces for us. We lived with my grandmother, and with love, happiness and pride—and the help of one devoted old housekeeper—she took care of her large family. Born in Ireland, she had come to the United States as a young bride in a very small ship when passengers usually brought extra food with them. She had been supplied by her mother with a good, nourishing blood pudding—but she never ate blood pudding again!

[4]

Her cooking was flavored with memories of her old home. It was said that her grandmother had raised the finest beef cattle in County Cork and was the only woman in Ireland who could skin a calf! My grandmother must have inherited something from hers, for she was particularly fussy about the quality of the meat she bought and had intricate discussions with the butcher about the proper way to cut a steak or roast of beef.

She preferred to do her own marketing, but occasionally she decided that I could do with a bit of training and let me go to the store for her.

I solemnly presented myself to the grocer to recite my order—"a shilling's worth of eggs [a dozen and a half eggs for 25 cents], a loaf of sugar [a 3½-pound solid cone of sugar wrapped in blue paper], rashers of bacon, a dip of milk [milk was sold from an open barrel and was dipped out into your own milk pail], a cake of 'east and a tin of treacle." A bit of the old country always lingered on in our household.

As a reward for doing the errand, I was allowed to fish out, with a sharp pointed stick, a big dill pickle from the wooden barrel in the back of the store.

My grandmother used to corn her own beef and also corned leg of lamb, which she served with a mustard sauce and mashed yellow turnips.

Her corned beef and cabbage and plain boiled potatoes made a divine dish—melting corned beef, simmered for hours with spices and herbs, and the potatoes cooked soft in madly boiling water, drained thoroughly, and then shaken in the pan over the heat until the "taters opened up and smiled at you." They were always snow white and floury, never damp and soggy.

My grandfather often did a bit of shopping on his way home, and when he stopped at the slaughterhouse on First Avenue where the United Nations Building now stands, he would bring home a treat—"the liver and the lights." That meant calves were being killed that day and he had bought a fresh calf's liver and sweetbreads. Sometimes he brought home tender little lambs' tongues, which were pickled and served with an egg sauce.

The calf's liver was left whole, larded with thin strips of salt pork, sprinkled with herbs and spices, covered with strips of bacon and roasted, being basted often with the bacon fat and plenty of melted butter. It was heavenly served hot with a purée of dried peas, or served cold next day with rye bread and mustard pickles.

If you were sick in our house, you went straight to bed with a "physic," and then came a cup of delicious beef tea with buttered toast. The beef tea was made from top round of beef cut into tiny cubes and was really a rich consommé. The cooked cubes of meat came right along with the beef tea.

Another invalid's drink was called fluffin—a handful of oatmeal or barley boiled in a quart of milk and flavored with nutmeg and sugar. If you were quite sick, you got a dash of the "real thing" in it, too—the best brandy was taken out of its hiding place for the occasion.

Soup was a great favorite in our house, for we were a large family of children, and soup and bread and butter could be counted on to fill us up. Most often it was the good old stand-by, beef and vegetable soup. My mother always hummed the recipe like a little tuneless song when she made it or else she would forget to put something in:

> *A shin of beef and bones,*
> *Pepper, salt, and onions,*
> *Carrots and celery,*
> *Bay leaf and parsley,*
> *Leeks and potatoes,*
> *A can of tomatoes,*
> *And a handful of oatmeal to stick to your ribs.*

How much of each thing? That's simple: just enough. If times were good, there was lots of everything and not too much water. If times were bad, there was lots of water and less of everything else, but it was always delicious.

The meaty shin of beef, with extra veal knuckle and marrow bones, was the main item. All the vegetables were cut up in small pieces, and the good handful of oatmeal flakes thickened up the soup a bit. Long, slow cooking for about four hours, and then big soup plates full of golden, fragrant liquid with slices of the tender boiled beef and all the vegetables served with it. It was eating and drinking too, we were always told.

When one of us had a birthday or deserved a reward for good behavior, we were allowed to choose some favorite dish, and mine was always "some of Grandma's soup."

When I was ten years old, I learned both to sew and cook. My grandmother said no one could cook without wearing an apron, so before I learned to cook I had to make my own aprons. All dolled up in my frilly, starched white apron, I started with baking-powder biscuits and then learned to make cream sauce without any lumps. Next came chocolate layer cake. The ten-year-old red-haired freckle-faced plump little girl was all eyes and ears at these lessons, and the chocolate cake was important, for it was her favorite dessert.

It was a two-egg yellow cake baked in two layers. I was taught how to separate the eggs and beat the yellows till really thick, not halfway, and beat the whites just right—careful, not too dry. Then, when the flour went in, no more beating, just careful folding. The two layers were cooled after baking and each was split so there would be more room for the soft, creamy chocolate filling—a sort of Irish Dobos torte.

Now my repertoire was complete from soup to dessert, and I looked forward to rainy days when I could wheedle my way into the kitchen because I couldn't go outdoors to play.

On would come supper all done by me, but inevitably it was my sole menu:

soup
baking-powder biscuits and
chocolate layer cake to end up with

Turkey time at Thanksgiving was a great treat—not because of the turkey, to my mind, but for the stuffing. I was so crazy about the stuffing that after the turkey was stuffed to bursting, an extra portion was wrapped loosely in a square of cheesecloth and tucked into the pan alongside the turkey. The rich turkey fat sizzled round my little bundle, and when the cheesecloth was opened up, there was a crisp golden ball with a soft, spicy, fragrant center, all for me.

Toast made over hot coals was something special. Orders were given by me every winter morning when I left for school: "Don't put any coal on the fire till after I get home" because after school the warm, happy kitchen meant homework at the kitchen table and "a bit of food to keep up a poor child's strength for study"—cups of sweet, milky tea and hot toast made over the glowing coals. I took the stove lid off and carefully inspected the fire. It mustn't have any little bluish licks of gassy flame, and the red embers had to

be just right. Out came the long toasting fork, the thick slice of bread was speared on carefully and held over the hot coals just high enough so as not to burn my fingers or the toast. Then, when the toast was golden brown, I spread it generously with sweet butter and back over the coals it went for just the right few seconds while I watched the golden liquid bubble and froth. Oh, perfection! No electric toaster can match it.

The Christmas dish was always a roast goose, and Grandma had to make several visits to the butcher to be sure we were getting a fine, plump, young "green goose." That meant this year's goose, not last year's—and no trying to put one over on Grandma. She knew what the young ones looked like: soft yellow feet and a soft yellow beak. She tweaked and pinched a dozen beaks before she decided which goose she wanted.

The goose was stuffed with a special potato stuffing— creamy mashed potatoes full of chopped onions which had been simmered in butter, dried bread crumbs, two beaten eggs and lots of sage and thyme, salt and pepper and the cooked giblets, chopped very fine.

The roasting was done in the hot oven of the coal stove. All the drafts were opened up and the oven was tested with a piece of white paper; the exact minutes necessary to brown the paper were carefully computed. Who needed an oven thermometer? The roasting was carefully watched, for the goose fat had to be spooned off several times as it cooked out. It mustn't be allowed to burn, for it was kept to be mixed with camphorated oil and rubbed on chests when we had coughing colds.

To go with the goose, red apples were cored but not peeled. Cut into thick slices, they were fried in butter and sprinkled with sugar.

Mashed turnips, which I hated, and cabbage went with the goose, and dessert was plum pudding. The goose was served on a special large platter which was called an ashet— a word still used in Ireland for a large platter. It must come from the French word for a plate, *assiette*.

We never had anything out of season, so when things were in season we enjoyed them every day, and it seems to me they were sweeter, more tender, more luscious and surely more appreciated than the all-year-round foods we have to-day. We looked forward to our seasonal treats and listened for the peculiar street cries of the sellers.

The fruit carts, gay with bright paint and flags and banners, and ringing bells or blowing whistles, came to the houses, and we knew the Rhubarb Man would come in the spring, the Strawberry Man in June and the Grape Man in September. Then what a doing there was!

In the spring we were dosed with rhubarb, sulfur and molasses, good for the blood! In June we had the Strawberry Festival; in September we had the Grape Cure for our "insides," as it was delicately explained.

We waited for the Peach Man and the Banana Man, who sold you a "hand" of bananas. In the summer the Pineapple Man came around and cut ripe, juicy pineapples into long, thin strips. The Watermelon Man would sell a big slab of juicy melon for a couple of pennies. Oranges appeared only at Christmastime in our stockings. Even today when I peel an orange on the Fourth of July, I think of Santa Claus and Christmas trees.

Another itinerant friend was the Coconut Man, who had pieces of fresh coconut for sale—hard on the teeth of a young one, but deliciously sweet and chewy, and a penny piece lasted quite a while. I seldom eat candy, but about twice a year I go on a coconut binge. Coconut bonbons and coconut kisses are my downfall.

The Strawberry Festival was put on to raise money for the Ladies' Aid Society. Everybody we knew bought tickets —twenty-five cents for children and fifty cents for grownups and you had a feast of all you could eat.

The menu was

fresh strawberries and cream
strawberry short cake
strawberry pie
strawberry ice cream
strawberry soup

The "soup" was just crushed berries and sugar and water, served in a cup, and I didn't think much of it! I suspect now that the grownups had a touch of something extra in theirs because their cups seemed to be refilled pretty often.

Not until the summer of 1961, when I was in Vienna, did I ever see strawberry soup again. At the Imperial Hotel there, I found "Strawberry Soup" on the menu. It was served as a first course, icy cold, and the crushed berries and sugar had been mixed with white wine slightly thickened with fine tapioca and flavored with a spot of something else (maybe brandy—I couldn't find out), and that's why I suspect the Ladies' Aid strawberry soup for the grownups was spiked. The Viennese version, incidentally, was wonderful!

I remember May parties in Central Park on the first day of May. All the girls wore gay colored crepe-paper dresses and danced around the Maypoles, winding ribbons around the poles and each other. Somebody supplied a big picnic lunch, but not for me. I was very fussy and didn't like anything not made at home. So I carried my lunch and, no matter how many May parties and outings I went to, my lunch was always the same—ham sandwiches on thickly buttered white bread, crusts cut off, no mustard; one pear, apple or banana; one cupcake with white icing; and lemonade in a bottle, usually with a slightly leaky cork. All in a cardboard shoebox—but tied with ribbon, not string! It was a Plain Jane kind of lunch—no fancy aluminum lunchbox or Thermos bottle to be cleaned. I ate the sandwiches, drank the lemonade and threw away the bottle, threw away the shoebox (but saved the ribbon!) and didn't have to worry about carrying things home. Very practical indeed.

In the kitchen alongside the coal range we had a gas stove for summer cooking. But very often in summer when it was too hot to cook or eat much, we would have just one wonderful dish for supper.

Strawberry shortcake in a deep soup plate with a warm,

crisp biscuit base, crushed sugar and berries ladled generously onto the biscuit and thick yellow cream poured on. No
foolish business about whipping the cream! In those days we
had to do that with a flat hand beater and it took too much
elbow grease, so we just poured on the cream as it came.

Blueberries with cinnamon toast were good. White bread
was toasted, lavishly buttered and sprinkled with cinnamon
sugar and put in a deep dish. Half the blueberries were
crushed and mixed with sugar and poured over the toast,
and the rest were left whole and put on top; then another
sprinkling of cinnamon sugar and heavy thick cream was
poured on.

Raspberries were made into flummery—a very soft rice
pudding with stewed raspberries and cream. Flummery was
made with all kinds of fruit.

With these summer dishes we drank milk or cold tea, and sometimes we drank ice-cold buttermilk with tiny golden flakes of butter floating in it.

We never had very fancy rich desserts. Mostly we ate fruit—sliced bananas sprinkled with lemon juice and brown sugar, prunes and apricots cooked together, applesauce, rhubarb stewed, berries of all kinds, melons, apples, pears and peaches.

In winter we had fruits that had been put up in jars during the summer.

Cakes were rather plain, but pound cake was a specialty.

This pound cake was the real thing, made of only four ingredients—a pound of butter whipped to a light cream; a pound of fine sugar added and whipped with the butter to frothy lightness; a pound of eggs, yolks beat up first and put into the butter and sugar; then a pound of flour gently sifted in. Egg whites, beaten till stiff, were folded in last, and a few drops of brandy or whisky gave flavor to the cake.

We always had a light supper the day the pound cake was made because the cook spent all afternoon whipping the batter by hand in a large yellow bowl which could eventually be scraped by a patiently waiting child.

The oven had to be loaded several times, for a dozen cakes would be made on these occasions. Wrapped in brandy-soaked clean linen napkins, they kept well for several weeks.

The cakes had no leavening but the egg whites and the air beaten in, but they rose up into golden mounds and split open in the middle just enough to give a soft uneven surface —not like today's machine-made, flat, dark brown, square-top cake.

My grandmother had a cousin who was full of airs and graces and fancied herself as a singer. The pound cake was always on hand for her visits, and the two Victorian ladies and I would sit on the spindly gilt chairs in the front parlor, drinking endless cups of tea and enjoying the pound cake.

The cousin would finally compliment the hostess on the superb cake, and only then would the hostess ask the guest to sing.

She would seat herself at the old square piano and, in a lovely contralto voice, sing Irish songs. They were always sad songs, about Kathleen Mavourneen, Mother Machree and a girl named Macushla, all of whom were pining away with broken hearts, and I would sit on my gilded chair, crying my eyes out for the lost loves of Irish lads and lassies. Because I felt so badly for the sorrows of Ireland, I would be given an extra piece of cake.

My other memory of pound cake is connected with September 3, 1939. Hitler had invaded Poland two days before. Always, when I am distressed, I have to keep very busy with my hands, and on that Sunday, upset by war news, I decided to mix a batch of pound cake. I was in the midst of it when the children ran into the kitchen to tell me there was special news on the radio, so I took my mixing bowl into the living room and continued to cream the butter and sugar while listening to the voice of the Prime Minister, Neville Chamberlain, declaring that England was at war with Germany.

Another favorite was what I called my "bread cake." A thick slice of crusty fresh bread was extravagantly buttered and spread thick with vanilla sugar. That solid cone of loaf sugar always had to be grated, and that was my job. Some was kept in a special glass with a vanilla bean, to be used just for cakes.

Hot gingerbread eaten with a dish of applesauce was good. The next day the leftover gingerbread was covered with a vanilla icing.

On Sundays or birthdays we had layer cakes with fancy fillings and frostings.

Milk puddings were not great favorites of mine. I always said they were too white! Rice puddings, junkets, cornstarch puddings, custards appeared in the winter.

[*14*]

We seldom had pies because my grandmother said she had "a heavy hand and foot for pastry."

Breakfasts were simple but filling. A good start means a good day. We never had fruit or fruit juice in the morning, but started right in on good stirabout, which was oatmeal porridge with a bit of butter melting on the hot surface and plenty of brown sugar and half cream, half milk—or cornmeal mush, or fried eggs and rashers (bacon), or pancakes and sausage cakes. Bread and butter, and jam on the side. Milk to drink in summer and weak tea in winter, but never coffee for the children. For that we had to sneak a taste from some indulgent aunt or uncle.

We never ate such a thing as a raw vegetable except sliced tomatoes—good heavens, no! You would have been considered "quite singular" if you did any such crazy thing.

I never saw a cookbook in our house, and I never saw my grandmother or my mother write anything down. So my family recipes come "out of my head"—just memories of how things tasted and looked, and that's the way I've cooked these favorites of ours all these years.

COUNTRY LIFE

AS I grew up, I tried more and more kinds of cooking. It became a hobby of mine, but never did I dream that it would lead to a business career in the food world.

At school I majored in mathematics and finance courses, and, fortunately for me, my business training started in a bank. Years later, when the Pepperidge Farm business began to expand, that banking experience was of tremendous value. I enjoyed six years of the banking and brokerage business before I married in 1923.

Then I really became serious about cooking.

My husband always has had a great sense of adventure and curiosity about everything. The result was that any whim or idea of his or mine usually became a real project, and we vied with each other for results.

One of our whimsical ideas was to live a real country life. In 1926 we bought 125 acres of land in Connecticut, part of which had once been a farm. One of the attractions of the place was a group of beautiful trees with unusually gorgeous coloring in the autumn, and when we discovered that they were a variety of the sourgum species and were known as pepperidge trees, we called the place Pepperidge Farm. We built a house and farm buildings and started our country life like babes-in-the-wood, for neither of us knew anything about country ways.

Pepperidge Farm really was a farm for us, and our first commercial venture was to put in an orchard of five hundred apple trees, which have been bearing beautiful apples for the past thirty years. I surely can tell you how to cook apples! We raised all our own vegetables, small fruits—pears, peaches and plums—and poultry—turkeys, chickens and capons. And we also raised three sons.

During the war we bravely tackled raising our own Porterhouse steaks and hams and bacon, which, by a miracle, turned out very well. We didn't know the first thing about it, but I wrote to the Department of Agriculture in Washington for the list of government pamphlets and ordered #1186, all about killing, curing and corning pork, and another one all about beef.

When the booklets came, we studied the instructions and were ready to try. We started off with a few baby pigs and one young steer, and when the pampered pigs and the fatted calf were in prime condition, the butcher came to slaughter them.

We equipped one farm building with refrigerating machinery so we could chill the meat properly at controlled temperatures. In addition, we put in a freezer room about six feet by ten feet, to be kept at ten degrees below zero so that after the meat had been properly prepared we could freeze it.

It really was very little trouble, and the quality of the meat was excellent.

The first lot of hams and bacon we did by the dry cure. We bought Dry Sugar Cure, read the instruction booklet and followed every word. But it was mighty hard, cold work in that chilly refrigerated building, and rubbing the salt into the pork made our hands purple and numb.

The next lot we did in brine, again following instructions, and that was much easier on us and made excellent products.

Pig's head is full of good meat, and our German gardener's wife always made delicious head cheese, or "souse," as she called it.

We made our own lard from the loin fat, sausage meat from all the small parts, and the liver was made into a pâté.

Our beef was really marvelous because we had good grass pastures and raised field corn for fattening up the cattle.

Like all husbands, mine became an expert at broiling steaks over charcoal—he likes to rub mustard over the surface and then sprinkle lightly with sugar, which burns off in the cooking but makes a nice crisp surface.

I always loved seeing a good supply of homemade foods in my store cupboards—jellies and jams from our own fruits, pickles and preserves, big crocks of our own sauerkraut, eggs kept in waterglass, and jars of my special mincemeat.

I'll never forget the first strawberry jam I made. I thought I might as well make a good big batch while I was at it, so I cleaned and hulled and crushed strawberries and sugar together for hours and filled up a huge pot. I stirred and stirred and thought it would never come to a boil. Well, it did—just when I had my back turned. Whoosh! Over the top it went, frothing and boiling all over the stove into sticky crimson puddles on the kitchen floor. That's how I discovered that small batches of jam cooked in a big pot come out better in more ways than one!

I must say I was very prideful about my homemade mincemeat, which always turned out well. The recipe was given to me when I was a bride by a very fussy friend of the family. She told me it was perfect just as it was, and I never made the slightest change in it, for she was right. For years and years on November 1st I made a big batch of it and put the filled jars away to ripen for Thanksgiving and Christmas.

In the early days at Pepperidge Farm we made our own sauerkraut. We had an old-fashioned hand cutter for the cabbage, which we placed over large earthenware crocks and shredded the cabbage right into them. Each layer of cabbage was sprinkled with salt, and when the crock was full, clean grape leaves were laid on the top and a plate with a big stone went on next to keep the cabbage under the brine which formed from the salt. A clean cheesecloth next, and then the crock was left to ferment.

When the sauerkraut was ready, we cooked it in various ways, sometimes with chopped onion and apple, sometimes with caraway seeds and tomatoes, and sometimes with stuffed cabbage rolls. A roast loin of pork with sauerkraut and applesauce is a grand dinner for a cold winter's evening.

During the war we made our own butter. As usual, I knew nothing about the subject, so again I wrote to Uncle Sam for a free booklet and found it very easy to follow instructions.

We bought a secondhand cream separator and a wooden barrel churn and made five pounds of butter at a time. We learned that a certain exact degree of temperature of the cream made the butter come very easily. Otherwise you might churn till your arm was stiff before you succeeded.

We were very popular during ration time because we

could always give a present of some precious butter or a bit of bacon to our friends.

During the sugar rationing I used to make icing for cakes by whipping egg whites with jam or jelly or orange marmalade. Delicious! But you had to eat it right away before the egg whites deflated.

Now our children are married and off in their own homes and there's no need for that big storeroom, but I sadly miss the pleasures of those busy years.

PEPPERIDGE FARM

IN 1937 the most amazing period of my life started purely by chance.

I had become intensely interested in the study of proper nutrition, particularly for young children. Searching for medical advice about treating a special allergic condition, I was told by an allergy specialist that a basic diet of natural foods was most important, not only for children but for adults as well. In some allergy cases the only flour or starch in the diet should be made from fresh, stone-ground, whole wheat.

The stone-ground whole-wheat flour was new to me. It contains the wheat germ, rich in the miraculous Vitamin B_1.

My husband and I worked out a diet that used only fresh fruits and vegetables, fresh meat and fish, natural sugars (honey and molasses) and the fresh, stone-ground, whole-wheat flour which I bought from an old New England gristmill—no white flour, no white sugar.

We used the flour first in delicious whole-wheat pancakes and muffins. Then, even though the flour seemed quite coarse in texture, I decided one day to try making some bread. I had never made a loaf of bread in my life, but I got out all the cookbooks I owned, read all the directions and started in. That first loaf should have been sent to the Smithsonian Institution as a sample of bread from the Stone Age, for it was hard as a rock and about one inch high. The trouble was that I had never before used yeast, which needs careful temperature control.

So I started over again. After a few more efforts by trial and error, and with a few competitive experiments by my husband, we achieved what seemed like good bread. I was generous in my use of butter and milk, honey and molasses, and invented a recipe which resulted in a delicious bread, pleasant for anyone to eat without being told "Eat it because it's good for you."

All the family liked it, and pretty soon we ate nothing but homemade whole-wheat bread. When I told the doctor I was making bread from the stone-ground flour, he wouldn't believe me because he said it was too coarse and I would have to add white flour to it. To convince him, I brought him some samples and told him exactly what I put in with the flour. Immediately he wanted to order it for himself and for his other patients.

I was quite taken aback by this idea, but I knew the bread was nutritious, unique, and delicious and was indeed an important part of the whole diet.

I decided to work only through doctors. Armed with a letter from my specialist, I approached three or four doctors. Before I realized what could happen, they began telling patients about my product, and very soon I had a sizable mail-order business.

I had to employ a young girl to help, and I taught her how to bake, for she had never made bread either. There we were on the farm in the hot August days of 1937, a pair of amateur bakers, mixing and kneading and baking like mad and then, when the loaves were cooled, making neat little packages to send by parcel post to our beloved customers. It was about the hottest summer I remember, and tears flowed when a batch of dough just didn't come out right and had to be discarded after all our toil and trouble.

That girl celebrated her twenty-fifth year with the Pepperidge Farm Company last summer. Soon I employed her sister, her brother, her sister-in-law, her cousins, and at one time ten members of her family were Pepperidge Farm employees. Some of the girls married, but there are six of the family with us now.

Now, all of this couldn't continue in my kitchen, so we moved ourselves into one of our farm buildings.

I believe that success is often the result of an accidental circumstance and an opportunity to take advantage of it. My accidental circumstance was my interest in proper food for children, and the opportunity to take advantage of it lay in the fact that we had space and facilities to work with, and a ready-made name for products from Pepperidge Farm.

In 1929, when we had built our house at Pepperidge Farm, my husband had also built a large garage and a large stable for his polo ponies. But in 1932, after a bad riding accident, polo and riding had had to be abandoned, and in 1937 we had lots of empty space to use.

First I walled off some space in the garage and made a nice room about twenty feet square, painted it pale green, hung up some curtains, put linoleum on the floor and installed a few pieces of equipment. Of course, this was all just a hobby, for I never dreamed of developing a business. I didn't spend a dollar if I could avoid it, and just used odds and ends I had in the house. I had a small gas stove in which we could make eight loaves at a time, an old table, a few mixing bowls, the old baby scale brought down from the attic to weigh the dough, a few bread pans and a few wire-mesh trays for cooling the bread. All these objects are now in the Pepperidge Farm Museum in one of our bakeries.

On we went with our mail-order business, and our operations soon took over all the space in the garage. Eventually we made the old stable building into a model bakery.

More and more friends and neighbors demanded our bread, so I decided to take a dozen loaves to our local grocer and ask if he would like to sell it. Regular commercial bread was then selling at ten cents a loaf, but I calmly announced that the price to him was twenty cents and that he could sell it at twenty-five. He told me later that he had thought I was just plain daft, but I was a good customer and he hadn't wanted to tell me he knew no one would pay that much for one loaf of bread.

I had thought that might be his reaction, however, so I had come prepared with some butter and a bread knife. I sliced a loaf and buttered the slices, and he and his clerks sampled my product. The look on their faces told the story. They all reached for more and said, "Well, that's bread!" I then gave my well-rehearsed sales talk about the ingredients I used and the high quality of the product and left my loaves. Before I got home my grocer friend had telephoned to say he was all sold out and wanted more.

Within a week people were talking about this new kind of bread, and every grocery store in our neighborhood called and wanted to sell our homemade product.

Up to November of 1937 we made only whole-wheat bread, but by then I thought there was also a market for old-fashioned white bread of fine quality for those people who preferred it to whole-wheat.

However, I would make it only of unbleached white flour, which very few commercial bakers were using because unbleached white flour must be slowly aged before it is ready for baking good bread. The chemical bleaching process had come into use because it not only made the flour super white but changed the baking quality of the flour in some way which eliminated the time needed for aging.

With the creamy-colored unbleached flour I used only honey as a sweetener, grade-A butter and fresh whole milk, salt and yeast—nothing to make it puff up and look big. The result was my loaf looked small, but it tasted good and people liked it.

By this time our New York City mail orders had grown to a size that was difficult to handle. I went into New York one day and walked into Charles and Company, the famous old food specialty shop.

My husband had always said, "When you want something go right to the top man." So I asked for the manager. The manager came out, looking rather skeptical, to see a woman with a package under her arm, another package in one hand (which was a quarter-pound of butter) and in the other hand a bread knife. I was petrified with fright, and he probably was also when he saw my knife—but I told him about my homemade bread and about the doctors' patients who were ready-made customers that I could send to him. He still looked skeptical.

But I said, "Can I give you a sample?" So we went into his office and I cut a slice, buttered it and gave it to him. As soon as he tasted it, he said, "My goodness, that's just the kind of bread my mother made when I was a boy." So, of course, I was in! He ordered twenty-four loaves a day, and I promised to tell the mail-order customers to come to the shop for their bread.

I went across the street to the Grand Central Station, and got on a train, just delighted with myself. But on the train I got to thinking, "My goodness, he said to get twenty-four loaves to him early tomorrow morning—how am I going to do that?" Then I thought, "It's all right, don't I have a commuting husband who goes on the train to Grand Central every morning? And what's a couple of packages between friends?"

When I reached home, the girls and I made the bread and packaged it, and I hid it behind the door. I didn't tell my husband anything that night, but just as he was about to leave in the morning, I said, "By the way, Henry, won't you just take this little package"—it weighed twenty-five pounds —"in to Grand Central and send it across the street to Charles and Company?" If he had stopped to argue, he would have missed the train, so off he went with the package.

For several weeks he and the package rode in the club car to Grand Central, where a porter met him and for twenty-five cents took the package across the street to Charles and Company. Orders increased, and soon Henry was taking two packages each day. Well, that was all right —he had two hands. But when we got to three packages a day, what were we going to do?

Then we discovered that the Railway Express people make a business of delivering packages, and we started doing business with them.

And so we grew at first from store to store by word-of-mouth praise from customers because people talked about this unusual product. Gradually, other stores began asking for some of our bread to sell.

There was no planning, no theory, just: What is necessary to do next? Well, let's do it and see what happens. It was fun.

After a few months I decided that the little loose sheets of paper on which I kept my records were not very businesslike, and a neighbor offered to come around and set up some books for me.

I said, "Fine—how long will it take?"

"Oh," he said, "about half a day."

He finished the little bookkeeping set-up for me, and when he was about to leave he said, "I think a store I know would love to sell the bread," and I said, "Good. I will hire you as a salesman. Take some samples with you." Off he went, and he came back in the evening so excited he could hardly talk. He'd opened ten stores!

And he was rarin' to go the next day, too, so I said, "Well, all right, go ahead, go ahead." And he kept right on going! He came for half a day in 1937 and stayed for twenty-four years.

When we appeared on the market there was nothing like our product; today we have many imitators, but I suppose imitation is the greatest form of flattery and I believe competition is good for us. It prevents complacency and keeps us alert.

By 1940 we needed far more space than we had on the farm, and we rented some buildings in Norwalk just for a year while we bought land and drew up plans for a real bakery. But the war came along and we had to stay in those buildings until it was over. And that was torture, because they became much too small as we grew. Completely inefficient, and really a headache.

Now, how did we get enough stone-ground flour from old mills as we grew? Well, there was only one way—to find several old mills and either give them enough grinding business to warrant improvements and additions or operate them ourselves. We have had four old grist mills restored to full activity.

Three of them, owned by other people, did grinding for us; one of them we run ourselves; and, in addition, we bought old grinding stones and built a mill right into our newest bakery, the one outside Chicago.

And there we efficiently grind our own whole-wheat flour right in the bakery, which is my dream for all the other plants someday.

By either grinding the whole-wheat flour ourselves or having it done under our close supervision, we control the freshness and quality of the flour—it is very important that this flour be kept cool during grinding and not heated by too rapid revolutions of the stones.

THE STORY OF BREAD

IT IS believed that wheat was growing in the highlands of Abyssinia about five thousand years ago. It must have been growing in Egypt also, for grains of wheat were found in an Egyptian pyramid tomb dating back to 3000 B.C.

Bread was used as currency in Egypt, and at one time the salary of the chief priest was paid in "fine loaves" as well as "coarse loaves." The "fine loaves" must have been made of fine or white flour from which all the rough bran had been sifted by the hand labor of slaves.

When the Romans invaded Egypt in 47 B.C. the use of wheat was brought back to Rome and its conquered countries. But the Romans didn't conquer the Germans, so perhaps that is why nowadays rye bread is more popular than wheat bread in Germany.

The early records of Egyptian life—around 3000 B.C.—show that the baking of bread was considered important. The supervisor of the royal bakeries enjoyed a position of privilege. White bread at one's table was a mark of luxury, for slaves were needed for the long labor of sifting out by hand all the roughage from the ground whole wheat.

In ancient times bread was used as an offering to the gods. Pliny the Elder told of an urn in a temple in Rome which was always full of fresh bread, taken by the temple visitors as a gift to the gods.

The Greeks and Romans made baking more of an art and changed from the flat loaves of the Egyptians. The Romans had strict laws, and every baker who sold bread underweight was fined and put in prison.

Since prehistoric times some form of bread made from grains has been man's staple article of diet. All civilizations have had breads and cereals as principal foods, especially where meat was scarce or was forbidden for religious reasons. Of all the grains, wheat and corn (maize) appear in all civilizations as man's favorites. Barley, oats, rye, rice and millet are ground for flour but have much less gluten content, so the bread made from them is heavy.

The hard seeds of the grains were probably chewed by the cave men, until someone thought of grinding the seeds between stones. The upper and nether millstones spoken of in the Bible were considered an important part of a man's fortune if he was lucky enough to own a set.

In making stone-ground whole-wheat flour today for Pepperidge Farm Bread we use the upper and nether millstones. The lower stone is rigid and the upper stone revolves. The surfaces of both stones are intricately ground to create the passage of air, so that the flour, as it is ground, is forced off the edge of the stone into a bin underneath. Today's process for milling white flour is just a refinement of the basic operation. To separate the rough husks from the ground grain, the sifter was invented. Sifting out the bran and roughage makes smooth flour.

Many superstitions refer to bread.

To drop a slice of bread buttered side up means you will have a visitor.

If you dream about bread, you will make money.

If by chance you must take the last slice of bread on the plate, you will be an old maid or a bachelor. On the other hand, it is also said that if a girl deliberately waits for the last slice, she is waiting for a handsome husband.

When you are moving, the very last thing to put in the moving van is a loaf of bread, and it must be the first thing off at the new house so there will always be food in your house.

A crust of bread in a newborn baby's crib will keep evil spirits away.

When traveling in dangerous country, a crust in your pocket serves as a good-luck charm.

The Mohammedans never cut bread with a knife, but break it.

In Russia guests were welcomed with bread and salt.

"He knows which side his bread is buttered on" means he's a pretty keen fellow.

"It's my bread and butter" refers to the source of your income.

"It's not my bread and butter" means something is not important to you.

Ben Franklin said, "Never spare the parson's wine or the baker's bread."

"He butters his bread on both sides" means an extravagant chap.

The Spanish say, "With bread, troubles are less."

WHOLE-WHEAT BREAD

In my opinion, bread made from fresh, stone-ground, whole-wheat flour offers the best nutrition and the best flavor. This flour is not easy to find, but it can be purchased by mail direct from small mills that advertise in home-type magazines or special food magazines.

Bread made from fresh whole-wheat flour has more nutritional qualities than bread made from highly refined, unenriched flour. This is because whole-wheat flour is just what its name implies—all of the wheat, including the wheat germ, which is rich in Vitamin B_1. But wheat germ is perishable, so whole-wheat flour must be used soon after grinding —otherwise the flour becomes rancid.

The bran and wheat germ are removed when white flour is made.

I don't say you must eat only whole-wheat bread. Eat some white bread, too, but be sure it is of high quality, made of unbleached flour and other good ingredients, and firm to the touch. For children, I think, it is important that at least half of the bread they eat should be whole-wheat bread made of fresh stone-ground flour.

MAKING BREAD

There are many recipes for yeast breads—white, whole-wheat, cornmeal, French bread, sour rye and sweet rye, raisin breads and spicy sweet breads.

A basic recipe for white bread or whole-wheat bread can have as many variations as you can find time to try.

There are a few simple rules to follow:

Wheat flour is best for bread making because of the gluten content of wheat. Gluten makes the dough elastic and allows it to expand as the gas bubbles are formed by the action of yeast.

Flour for bread is made from hard wheat, and flour for cake is made from soft wheat. Flour from most other grains should be mixed with some wheat flour in order to get the action of the gluten.

All ingredients should be of the best quality.

Flour for white bread should be unbleached.

Flour for whole-wheat bread should be 100-percent fresh stone-ground hard-wheat flour used not more than two weeks after grinding and kept in a cool place, preferably in a refrigerator.

Originally housewives made their own yeast by fermenting potatoes or by using hops, but nowadays the packaged, dry, granulated yeast made by the various yeast companies is an excellent product and can be kept in your supply closet for at least a month. The amount of yeast to be used depends upon the length of time you want the dough to rise. A small amount of yeast will require a longer rising time. The directions on the yeast packages are very clear and easy to follow.

Water for dissolving dry yeast should feel very warm but not hot when tested on the inside of the wrist—about 105° F.

If you cannot buy dry yeast, use compressed yeast, which comes in one-ounce cakes. Water for compressed yeast need be only lukewarm—about 90° F.

All other ingredients and utensils should be at room temperature or even warmer.

Mixing bowls should be warmed by rinsing with hot water.

Stone-ground whole-wheat flour, when taken from a cool place, should be warmed slightly in a warm oven before mixing.

Butter or shortening should be melted and cooled before it is added to the mix.

Sugar and salt should be well dissolved in the warm liquid before flour is added to the mix.

Liquid can be all water or all milk or part of each.

After mixing and kneading, the dough should be covered with a damp cloth to prevent the surface from drying out and left to rise in a warm place, about 85° F., until double in bulk.

If it is difficult to find a place which is warm enough for dough to rise in the designated time, one of the following methods may be used.

1. Place the covered bowl of dough in a pan of warm water (about 87° F.); or

2. Heat water to the boiling point in a saucepan and remove from the heat. Place a rack, pie tin or cookie sheet over the pan. Place the covered bowl of dough on this support.

3. Experiment with your stove. Although stoves vary, a slightly warmed oven may be used to raise the dough. Use a thermometer to check the temperature, keeping the oven not over 85° F.

The proper size for a bread pan is about 9 inches long, 5 inches wide and 3 inches deep.

The pan can be greased with butter or any other shortening.

Pans should be cleaned thoroughly of grease after each baking.

When you start mixing the flour into the liquid, use a strong, long-handled mixing spoon so you can really beat the batter while it is soft.

As you add the last of the flour, the batter becomes a thick dough and then you can use your hands to knead in all of the flour.

KNEADING

The purpose of kneading is to distribute evenly by pressure all the air holes which are formed in the dough by the gas-producing action of yeast.

Kneading is not difficult.

For the first kneading after the ingredients have been well mixed, place the mixed ball of dough on a lightly floured board, flatten it into a circle with your hands to a thickness of about one inch and fold the top one third of the dough toward you.

On the doubled-over dough, press down and push away from you with the heels of your hands.

Give the dough a quarter-turn to the right and fold the next top in toward you, pressing down and pushing the folded dough away from you.

Continue turning, folding and kneading for at least five minutes until the dough feels smooth and elastic.

Form into a ball and replace in the bowl to rise in a warm place. Keep the bowl covered.

For the second kneading, after the dough has risen to double in bulk, divide the dough according to the number of loaves you are making. Knead each piece about three minutes and then shape into loaves to fit your pans.

Most recipes make two loaves, but with a bread-mixing pail you can easily make six or eight at one mixing and put the extra loaves, properly wrapped, in your freezer. This is a great time saver.

RECIPES

WHITE BREAD
(Makes 1 loaf)

Preheat oven to 400° F., 20 minutes before loaf is ready to bake.

½ cup milk
1 tablespoon sugar
1 teaspoon salt
4 teaspoons shortening or butter
½ cup warm water
1 package or cake yeast, dry or compressed
3 cups sifted white flour

Scald the milk.
Add and stir in the sugar, salt and shortening or butter.
Cool to lukewarm.
Measure into a large mixing bowl the warm (not hot) water.
(Cool to lukewarm for compressed yeast.)
Sprinkle or crumble in the yeast.
Stir until dissolved.
Add the lukewarm milk mixture.
Add and stir in 1½ cups sifted flour.
Beat until smooth.
Add and stir in an additional 1½ cups sifted flour (about).
Turn out on a lightly floured board.
Knead quickly and lightly until smooth and elastic.
Place in a greased bowl; brush lightly with melted shortening or butter.
Cover with a clean damp towel.
Let rise in a warm place, free from draft, until doubled in bulk, about 50 minutes.
Punch down.
Shape into a loaf and place in a greased bread pan, 9 by 5 by 3 inches.
Cover with a clean damp towel.
Let rise in a warm place, free from draft, until doubled in bulk, about 50 minutes.
Bake in a hot oven (400° F.) for about 50 minutes.

WHITE BATTER BREAD

(Makes 2 loaves)

Preheat oven to 375° F., 20 minutes before loaves are ready to bake.

1 cup milk
3 tablespoons sugar
1 tablespoon salt
2 tablespoons butter or margarine
1 cup very warm water
2 packages or cakes yeast, dry or compressed
4¼ cups unsifted flour

Scald the milk; stir in the sugar, salt and butter or margarine.
Cool to lukewarm.
Measure the very warm water into a large warm bowl.
Sprinkle or crumble in the yeast; stir until dissolved.
Add the lukewarm milk mixture.
Stir in the flour; the batter will be fairly stiff.
Beat until well blended, about 2 minutes.
Cover with a clean damp towel.
Let rise in a warm place, free from draft, until more than doubled in bulk, about 40 minutes.
Stir the batter down.
Beat vigorously, about ½ minute.
Turn into 2 greased loaf pans, 9 by 5 by 3 inches.
Bake in a moderate oven (375° F.) for about 50 minutes.

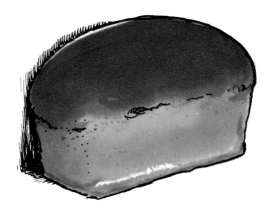

WHITE BREAD (Sponge Method)
(Makes 2 loaves)

Preheat oven to 400° F., 20 minutes before loaves are ready to bake.

1½ cups very warm water
2 tablespoons sugar
2 packages or cakes yeast, dry or compressed
7 cups unsifted *flour or 7½ cups sifted flour*
1 cup milk
2 tablespoons sugar
1 tablespoon salt
3 tablespoons butter or margarine

Measure the very warm water and sugar into a large bowl.
Sprinkle or crumble in the yeast.
Stir until dissolved.
Add 1½ cups *unsifted* flour or 2 cups sifted flour.
Beat until smooth.
Cover; let rise in a warm place, free from draft, until light and spongy, about 30 minutes.
Scald the milk; stir in the sugar, salt and butter or margarine; cool to lukewarm.
Stir the sponge down.
Stir in the lukewarm milk mixture and enough remaining flour to form a soft dough.
Turn out on a lightly floured board and knead until smooth and elastic, about 8 to 10 minutes.
Place in a greased bowl, turning to grease all sides.
Cover; let rise in a warm place, free from draft, until doubled in bulk, about 30 minutes.
Punch down.
Divide in half.
Shape into loaves.
Place in 2 greased bread pans, 9 by 5 by 3 inches.
Cover; let rise in a warm place, free from draft, until doubled in bulk, about 30 minutes.
Bake in a hot oven (400° F.) for about 50 minutes.
Remove from the pans and place on wire racks to cool.

STANDARD WHITE BREAD
(Makes 2 loaves)

Preheat oven to 400° F., 20 minutes before loaves are ready to bake.

½ cup milk
3 tablespoons sugar
2 teaspoons salt
3 tablespoons butter or margarine
1½ cups warm water
1 package or cake yeast, dry or compressed
5½ cups unsifted *flour (about)* or *6¼ cups sifted*
flour (about)

Scald the milk; stir in the sugar, salt and butter or margarine. Cool to lukewarm.

Measure the warm water into a large bowl; sprinkle or crumble in the yeast.

Stir until dissolved.

Add the lukewarm milk mixture and 3 cups flour; beat until smooth.

Add enough additional flour to make a soft dough.

Turn out onto a lightly floured board.

Knead until smooth and elastic, about 8 to 10 minutes.

Form into a smooth ball.

Place in a greased bowl, turning to grease all sides.

Cover; let rise in a warm place, free from draft, until doubled in bulk, about 1 hour.

Punch down.

Let rest for 15 minutes.

Divide the dough in half.

Shape each half into a loaf.

Place each loaf in a greased bread pan, 9 by 5 by 3 inches.

Cover; let rise in a warm place, free from draft, until doubled in bulk, about 1 hour.

Bake in a hot oven (400° F.) for about 50 minutes.

WHITE BREAD (QUICK METHOD)

(Makes 4 loaves)

Preheat oven to 400° F., 20 minutes before loaves are ready to bake.

2 cups milk
5 tablespoons sugar
2 tablespoons salt
2 packages dry yeast
2 cups warm water
12–13 cups sifted flour
5 tablespoons melted shortening or butter

Scald the milk; add the sugar and salt; cool to lukewarm.

Dissolve the yeast in warm (not hot) water and add to the lukewarm milk.

Add half the flour and beat until smooth.

Add the melted shortening or butter and the remaining flour, or enough to make an easily handled dough.

Knead the dough quickly and lightly until smooth and elastic.

Place the dough in a greased bowl.

Cover and let rise in a warm place, free from draft, until doubled in bulk, about 1½ hours.

When light, divide into 4 equal portions and shape into loaves.

Place in greased loaf pans.

Cover and let rise again until doubled in bulk, about 1 hour.

Bake in a hot oven (400° F.) for 15 minutes; then reduce heat to moderate (375° F.) and bake for about 30 minutes longer.

SALT-FREE WHITE BREAD
(Makes 1 loaf)

Preheat oven to 400° F., 20 minutes before loaf is ready to bake.

½ cup milk
1½ tablespoons sugar
4 teaspoons shortening or butter
½ cup warm water
1 package or cake yeast, dry or compressed
3 cups sifted white flour

Scald the milk.
Add and stir in the sugar and shortening or butter.
Cool to lukewarm.
Measure into a bowl the warm (not hot) water.
(Cool to lukewarm for compressed yeast.)
Sprinkle or crumble in the yeast.
Stir until dissolved.
Add the lukewarm milk mixture.
Add and stir in the flour.
Turn out on a lightly floured board.
Knead quickly and lightly until smooth and elastic.
Place in a well-greased bowl.
Brush lightly with melted shortening or butter.
Cover with a clean damp towel.
Let rise in a warm place, free from draft, until doubled in bulk, about 35 minutes.
Punch down.
Shape into a loaf.
Place in a well-greased bread pan, 9 by 5 by 3 inches.
Cover with a clean damp towel.
Let rise in a warm place, free from draft, until doubled in bulk, about 45 minutes.
Bake in a hot oven (400° F.) for about 50 minutes.

CASSEROLE WHITE BREAD

(Makes 2 loaves)

Preheat oven to 375° F., 20 minutes before loaves are ready
to bake.

1 cup milk
3 tablespoons sugar
1 tablespoon salt
1½ tablespoons shortening or butter
1 cup very warm water
2 packages dry yeast
4½ cups sifted flour

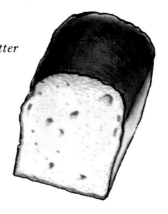

Scald the milk; stir in the sugar, salt and shortening or
butter.

Cool to lukewarm.

Measure the very warm water into a bowl.

Sprinkle in the yeast; stir until dissolved.

Add the lukewarm milk mixture and flour.

Stir until well blended, about 2 minutes.

Cover.

Let rise in a warm place, free from draft, until more than
doubled in bulk, about 40 minutes.

Stir the batter down.

Beat vigorously for about ½ minute.

Turn into a greased 1½-quart casserole or 2 greased loaf
pans, 9 by 5 by 3 inches.

Bake uncovered in a moderate oven (375° F.) for about 1
hour.

BUTTERMILK BREAD
(Makes 2 loaves)

Preheat oven to 375° F., 20 minutes before loaves are ready to bake.

1 cup buttermilk
3 tablespoons sugar
2½ teaspoons salt
⅓ cup margarine or butter
1 cup very warm water
1 package or cake yeast, dry or compressed
5¾ cups sifted flour (about)
¼ teaspoon baking soda

Scald the buttermilk (it will appear curdled); stir in the sugar, salt and margarine or butter.

Cool to lukewarm.

Measure the very warm water into a large bowl.

Sprinkle or crumble in the yeast.

Stir until dissolved.

Add the lukewarm milk mixture.

Stir in 3 cups sifted flour and the baking soda.

Beat until smooth.

Add the remaining 2¾ cups flour; use a little more or less, depending on the flour, to make a dough that has a rough, dull appearance and is a bit sticky.

Turn the dough out on a lightly floured board and knead until smooth and elastic (about 8 to 10 minutes).

Form into a ball and put into a greased bowl, turning to grease all sides.

Cover with a clean damp cloth and let rise in a warm place, free from draft, for about 1 hour, or until doubled in bulk.

Punch down, turn out on a lightly floured board and let rest for about 15 minutes.

Divide the dough in half.

Shape into loaves and place in 2 greased bread pans, 9 by 5 by 3 inches.

Cover and let rise in a warm place, free from draft, for about 1 hour, until doubled in bulk.

Bake in a moderate oven (375° F.) for about 35 minutes.

CORN BREAD

(Makes 2 loaves)

Preheat oven to 375° F., 20 minutes before loaves are ready to bake.

1 cup milk
6 tablespoons sugar
2 teaspoons salt
½ cup (1 stick) margarine or butter
½ cup warm water
2 packages or cakes yeast, dry or compressed
2 eggs, beaten
3½ cups unsifted *flour or 4¼ cups* sifted *flour*
1¾ cups yellow cornmeal

Scald the milk; stir in the sugar, salt and margarine or butter. Cool to lukewarm

Measure the warm water into a large bowl.

Sprinkle or crumble in the yeast; stir until dissolved.

Stir in the lukewarm milk mixture, beaten eggs, flour and cornmeal.

Beat until well blended, about 2 minutes.

The batter will be stiff.

Turn into 2 greased 8-inch round cake-layer pans or 2 greased loaf pans, 9 by 5 by 3 inches.

Cover and let rise in a warm place, free from draft, until doubled in bulk, about 1 hour.

Bake in a moderate oven (375° F.) for 30 to 35 minutes.

Serve warm.

WHEAT-GERM BREAD

(Makes 2 loaves)

Preheat oven to 400° F., 20 minutes before loaves are ready to bake.

1¼ cups water
3 tablespoons sugar
4 teaspoons salt
⅓ cup shortening or butter
⅓ cup molasses
¾ cup milk
1 cup wheat germ
¼ cup warm water
2 packages or cakes yeast, dry or compressed
4 cups unsifted whole-wheat flour
2 cups sifted white flour

In a saucepan combine 1¼ cups water and the sugar, salt, shortening or butter, and molasses.

Heat until the shortening melts.

Cool to lukewarm.

Scald the milk.

Pour the scalded milk over the wheat germ.

Let stand until the liquid is absorbed and the mixture has cooled to lukewarm.

Measure into a bowl ¼ cup warm (not hot) water.

(Cool to lukewarm for compressed yeast.)

Sprinkle or crumble in the yeast.

Stir until dissolved.

Add and stir in the lukewarm molasses mixture and the lukewarm wheat-germ mixture.

Add and stir in half of the mixed whole-wheat and white flour.

Beat until smooth.

Add and stir in the remaining flour mixture.

Turn the dough out on a lightly floured board.

Knead quickly and lightly until smooth and elastic.

[52]

Place in a greased bowl and brush the top lightly with melted shortening or butter.

Cover with a clean damp towel.

Let rise in a warm place, free from draft, until doubled in bulk, about 1½ hours; punch down and divide into 2 equal portions.

Shape into loaves and place in 2 greased bread pans, 9 by 5 by 3 inches.

Cover with a clean damp towel.

Let rise in a warm place, free from draft, until doubled in bulk, about 1¼ hours.

Bake at 400° F. for about 50 minutes.

HUNGARIAN CHRISTMAS BREAD
(Makes 4 loaves)

Preheat oven to 350° F., 20 minutes before loaves are ready to bake.

1 cup milk
½ cup sugar
1 teaspoon salt
1 cup (2 sticks) butter or margarine
⅓ cup very warm water
2 packages or cakes yeast, dry or compressed
5½ cups sifted flour (about)
grated rind of 2 lemons (2 tablespoons)

For the filling
2 cups ground poppy seeds
2 cups sugar
1 cup raisins
1 cup milk
grated rind of 2 lemons (2 tablespoons)
⅛ teaspoon powdered saffron (optional)
1 egg, beaten

Scald the milk; stir in the sugar, salt and butter or margarine. Cool to lukewarm.

Measure the very warm water into a large bowl and sprinkle or crumble in the yeast.

Stir in the lukewarm milk mixture.

Add 3 cups flour and the lemon rind.

Beat until smooth.

Add enough remaining flour to form a soft dough.

Turn out onto a lightly floured board and knead until smooth and elastic, about 8 to 10 minutes.

Put in a greased bowl, turning to grease all sides.

Cover and let rise in a warm place, free from draft, for about 1 hour, or until doubled in bulk.

Meanwhile prepare the filling.

[54]

Combine the ground poppy seeds, sugar, raisins, milk, lemon rind and saffron.

Mix well.

Cook this mixture, stirring constantly, over medium heat for about 10 minutes, or until thick enough to spread.

The mixture will thicken on standing.

Punch down the dough and divide into 4 equal parts.

Roll out each part into a rectangle ¼ inch thick.

Spread each rectangle with ⅔ cup filling and roll up like a jelly roll.

Place on greased baking sheets, seam side down, and brush with ½ the beaten egg.

Cover and let rise in a warm place, free from draft, for 30 minutes.

Brush with the remaining beaten egg.

Bake in a moderate oven (350° F.) for about 35 minutes, or until golden brown.

Remove from the baking sheets and cool.

OLD-FASHIONED POTATO LOAVES
(Makes 2 loaves)

Preheat oven to 400° F., 20 minutes before loaves are ready to bake.

1 medium potato
1 cup milk
2 tablespoons sugar
2 teaspoons salt
2 tablespoons butter or margarine
½ cup very warm water
2 packages or cakes yeast, dry or compressed
6 cups sifted flour (about)

Peel and dice the potato; boil in water to cover until tender, about 15 minutes.

Drain, reserving ½ cup liquid; mash and cool.

Scald the milk; stir in the sugar, salt, butter or margarine and reserved potato water; cool to lukewarm.

Measure the very warm water into a large bowl.

Sprinkle or crumble in the yeast; stir until dissolved.

Stir in the mashed potato, the lukewarm milk mixture and 3 cups flour; beat until smooth.

Stir in remaining flour to make a soft dough.

Turn out onto a lightly floured board.

Knead until smooth and elastic, about 8 minutes.

Place in a greased bowl, turning to grease all sides.

Cover; let rise in a warm place, free from draft, until doubled in bulk, about 35 minutes.

Punch down; turn the dough over in the bowl; cover and let rise again for about 20 minutes.

Punch down.

Turn out onto a lightly floured board; divide in half.

Shape each half into a loaf; place in 2 greased pans, 9 by 5 by 3 inches.

Cover; let rise in a warm place, free from draft, until the centers of the loaves are slightly higher than the sides of the pans, about 25 minutes.

Dust the loaves with flour.

Bake in a hot oven (400° F.) for 15 minutes; reduce the temperature to moderate (350° F.) and continue baking for about 30 minutes, or until done.

Remove from the pans; cool on wire racks or across the tops of the pans.

SALLY LUNN

(Makes 2 8-inch squares)

Preheat oven to 400° F., 20 minutes before squares are ready to bake.

1 cup milk
¼ cup sugar
2 teaspoons salt
½ cup (1 stick) butter or margarine
½ cup very warm water
1 cake or package yeast, dry or compressed
3 eggs, well beaten
5 cups sifted or 4½ cups unsifted flour
¼ cup sugar to sprinkle on surface

Scald the milk; add ¼ cup sugar, the salt and the butter or margarine.

Cool to lukewarm.

Measure the very warm water into a large bowl.

Sprinkle or crumble in the yeast.

Stir to dissolve.

Add the lukewarm milk mixture, eggs and flour; beat until smooth.

Cover; let rise in a warm place, free from draft, until doubled in bulk, about 1 hour.

Stir down, pour into 2 well-greased 8-inch-square cake pans.

Cover, let rise in a warm place, free from draft, until doubled in bulk, about 30 minutes.

Sprinkle each bread with 2 tablespoons sugar.

Bake in a hot oven (400° F.) for 25 minutes.

SOUPER-DOOPER BREAD
(Serves 8–10)

Preheat oven to 400° F., 20 minutes before bread is ready to bake.

2 packages or cakes yeast, dry or compressed
⅓ cup very warm water
1 can (10½ ounces) condensed onion soup
1 teaspoon salt
½ cup margarine or butter, softened
3½ cups sifted flour
grated cheese or sesame seeds

Sprinkle or crumble the yeast into the very warm water.
Stir until dissolved.
Stir in the onion soup.
Add the salt, the softened margarine or butter and 2 cups flour.
Beat until well blended.
Add the remaining flour and stir until blended.
Cover.
Let rise in a warm place, free from draft, for 1 hour.
Stir down.
Put into a greased 9-inch-square pan.
Spread the batter evenly.
Sprinkle the top with grated cheese or sesame seeds.
Cover.
Let rise in a warm place, free from draft, for 30 minutes.
Bake in a hot oven (400° F.) for 30 to 35 minutes.

QUICK-RISING SWEET DOUGH

¾ cup milk
½ cup sugar
1½ teaspoons salt
½ cup (1 stick) margarine or butter
¾ cup very warm water
3 packages or cakes yeast, dry or compressed
2 eggs, beaten
5½ cups unsifted flour (about)

Scald the milk; stir in the sugar, salt and butter or margarine; cool to lukewarm.

Measure the very warm water into a large bowl.

Sprinkle or crumble in the yeast; stir until dissolved.

Stir in the lukewarm milk mixture, the eggs and 3 cups flour; beat until smooth.

Stir in additional flour to make a soft dough.

Turn dough out onto a floured board; knead until smooth and elastic, about 8 minutes.

Place the dough in a greased bowl; turn the dough to grease it on all sides.

Cover; let rise in a warm place, free from draft, until doubled in bulk, about 30 minutes.

Punch the dough down and turn out onto a lightly floured board.

Proceed according to directions for the desired shapes (p. 86).

COCONUT COFFEE CAKE
(Makes 2 cakes)

Preheat oven to 350° F., 20 minutes before cakes are ready to bake.

Prepare 1 recipe Basic Sweet Dough (below).

½ cup margarine or butter
2 cups confectioner's sugar
2 tablespoons water
1 cup flaked coconut
1 egg yolk
2 tablespoons milk

When doubled in bulk, punch down and turn out on a lightly floured board; divide into 2 equal pieces.

Roll out each piece into a square of dough 14 by 14 by ⅛ inches.

Cream in a bowl the margarine or butter.

Beat in until smooth the sugar and the water.

Spread half of the mixture evenly on each square of dough.

Sprinkle evenly over each square ½ cup flaked coconut.

Roll up each piece as for a jelly roll.

Place on large greased baking sheets.

Shape into circles and seal the ends together firmly.

Flatten each slightly with the palm of your hand.

In each circle, with a sharp knife, make 2 circular cuts around the top about ¾ inch apart, penetrating to, but not through, the bottom layer of dough.

Cover with a clean damp towel.

Let rise in a warm place, free from draft, until doubled in bulk.

Beat together the egg yolk and the milk.

Brush the rings with the egg-and-milk mixture.

Bake in a moderate oven (350° F.) for about 30 minutes.

Sprinkle the tops while hot with confectioner's sugar.

BASIC SWEET DOUGH—NO KNEAD

(Yield: According to shape or shapes selected)

¾ cup milk
⅓ cup sugar
1 teaspoon salt
⅓ cup margarine or butter
½ cup very warm water
2 packages or cakes yeast, dry or
    compressed
3 eggs, beaten
5½ cups sifted *flour* or 4½ cups
    unsifted *flour*

Scald the milk.
Stir in the sugar, salt and margarine or butter.
Cool to lukewarm.
Measure the very warm water into a large bowl.
Sprinkle or crumble in the yeast.
Stir until dissolved.
Add the lukewarm milk mixture, eggs and flour.
Stir until well blended.
Cover.
Chill in the refrigerator for 2 hours or overnight.
Turn out onto a lightly floured board.
Proceed according to directions for the shapes selected (p. 86).

APPLE ORCHARD DELIGHT

Preheat oven to 375° F., 20 minutes before cake is ready to bake.

1 package dry yeast or 1 cake compressed
yeast
¼ cup warm (not hot) water
1 cup milk, scalded
2 tablespoons shortening or butter
2 tablespoons sugar
1 teaspoon salt
1 egg, beaten
3½ cups sifted flour
½ cup sugar
2 teaspoons cinnamon
1½ cups canned drained apple slices
½ cup broken walnuts or pecans
½ cup raisins
1 egg yolk, beaten
1 tablespoon water

Dissolve the yeast in the warm water.

Combine the milk, shortening or butter, 2 tablespoons sugar and the salt; cool to lukewarm.

Add the yeast and the beaten egg.

Mix well.

Gradually stir in flour to make a soft dough.

Beat vigorously until the dough forms a smooth, satiny ball.

Place in a greased bowl, turn once, cover and let rise until double in size in a warm place (about 1 hour).

Remove the dough, place on a lightly floured board and roll to an oblong shape 12 by 18 inches.

Sprinkle with a mixture of ½ cup sugar and the cinnamon.

Now place the apple slices in rows parallel to the 12-inch edges.

Sprinkle the raisins and nuts evenly to cover the dough.

Roll lengthwise as for a jelly roll.

Place on a greased baking sheet and shape into a ring.

Brush the ring with a mixture of the egg yolk and 1 tablespoon water.

Cover and let rise in a warm place 1 hour.

Bake at 375° F. for 30 minutes.

Decorate with Confectioner's-Sugar Icing (see below), candied cherries and nuts.

Confectioner's-Sugar Icing

Blend together 1½ cups sifted confectioner's sugar, ½ teaspoon flavoring (vanilla, lemon or almond) and about 1½ tablespoons water.

DOUBLE CHOICE CAKES

Preheat oven to 375° F., 20 minutes before cakes are ready to bake.

> ⅓ cup milk
> ½ cup sugar
> 1 teaspoon salt
> 2 packages or cakes yeast, dry or
>   compressed
> ½ cup very warm water
> 3½ cups sifted flour
> ½ cup margarine or butter
> 2 eggs, beaten
> 1½ teaspoons grated orange rind

Scald the milk; add ¼ cup sugar and the salt; cool to luke-warm.

Sprinkle or crumble the yeast into the very warm water; stir until dissolved.

Add the milk mixture and 1 cup flour; beat until smooth.

Cover; let rise in a warm place, free from draft, until light, about 20 minutes.

Cream the margarine or butter until light and fluffy.

When the yeast mixture is light, beat in the margarine or butter, ¼ cup sugar, the eggs and the orange rind with a wooden spoon.

Stir in the remaining 2½ cups flour; beat hard.

Divide the batter in half.

Orange Loaf

Turn half the batter into a well-greased loaf pan, 9 by 5 by 3 inches.

Cover.

Let rise in a warm place, free from draft, about 1 hour.

Bake in a moderately hot oven (375° F.) for 30 minutes.

When cool, top with an Orange Glaze (below).

Orange Glaze

Add 1 teaspoon grated orange rind and 2 tablespoons orange juice to 1 cup confectioner's sugar.

Beat thoroughly.

Fruit Cake

Toss together ½ cup raisins, ½ cup chopped walnuts, ½ cup chopped candied fruit, ½ teaspoon cinnamon, ½ teaspoon ginger and ¼ teaspoon nutmeg.

Add to the remaining batter and blend well.

Turn into a well-greased mold.

Cover.

Let rise in a warm place, free from draft, about 1½ hours.

Bake in a moderately hot oven (375° F.) for 30 to 35 minutes.

If desired, frost with Confectioner's-Sugar Icing (p. 63).

FRESH PEACH KUCHEN

(Makes 1 9-inch cake)

Preheat oven to 350° F., 20 minutes before cake is ready to bake.

½ cup milk
½ cup warm water
¼ cup margarine or butter
2 packages dry yeast or 2 cakes
   compressed yeast
3½ cups sifted flour
⅓ cup sugar
1½ teaspoons salt
1 egg

For the topping:
½ cup flour
⅓ cup sugar
½ cup chopped pecans.
¼ cup margarine or butter
1½ teaspoons cinnamon
2 large peaches, pared and sliced

Scald the milk; remove from heat.

Add the warm water, margarine or butter, and yeast. Stir until dissolved.

Measure the flour, sugar and salt into a large mixing bowl.

Add the beaten egg and the milk mixture.

Stir until well blended.

Cover; let rise in a warm place, free from draft, until doubled in bulk, about 1 hour.

Meanwhile rub together the flour, sugar, chopped pecans, margarine or butter and cinnamon until crumbly.

Stir the dough down and spread evenly in a greased 9-inch-square pan.

Arrange the peach slices on top and sprinkle with the crumbly mixture.

Let rise in a warm place, free from draft, until doubled in bulk, about 40 minutes.

Bake in a moderate oven (350° F.) for 35 minutes.

FRESH APPLE KUCHEN
(Makes 1 9-inch cake)

Preheat oven to 375° F., 20 minutes before cake is ready to bake.

¼ cup very warm water
1 package or cake yeast, dry or compressed
½ cup (1 stick) margarine or butter
½ cup sugar
½ teaspoon salt
3 eggs
¼ cup milk
2¾ cups sifted flour

Measure the very warm water into a small bowl.

Sprinkle or crumble in the yeast; stir until dissolved.

Cream the margarine or butter thoroughly in a large electric-mixer bowl.

Gradually add the sugar and salt; cream together.

Add the dissolved yeast, eggs and milk; beat at medium speed until well blended.

Gradually add and blend in the flour while beating at medium speed; beat until the mixture is well blended.

Spread the dough in a well-greased square pan, 9 by 9 by 2 inches.

Arrange Apple Topping (below) on top.

Cover.

Let rise in a warm place, free from draft, until doubled in bulk, about 1 hour.

Bake in a moderate oven (375° F.) for about 40 minutes.

Turn out of the pan and cool on a wire rack.

Serve warm.

For the topping:
2 cups fresh apple slices
⅔ cup sugar
6 tablespoons butter or margarine
½ cup flour
2 tablespoons cinnamon

Arrange the fresh apple slices on top of the batter.

Mix together until crumbly the sugar, butter or margarine, flour and cinnamon.

Sprinkle over the apples.

APPLE CAKE
(Makes 2 8-by-12-inch cakes)

Preheat oven to 400° F., 20 minutes before cakes are ready to bake.

> *½ cup milk*
> *½ cup sugar*
> *¼ teaspoon salt*
> *¼ cup (½ stick) butter or margarine*
> *½ cup very warm water*
> *2 packages or cakes yeast, dry or compressed*
> *2 eggs, beaten*
> *4¾ cups sifted flour (about) or 3¾ cups*
> *   unsifted flour (about)*
> *melted margarine or butter*
> *1¼ cup sugar*
> *8 to 10 medium-size apples*
> *1½ teaspoons cinnamon*

Scald the milk; stir in the salt, butter or margarine and ½ cup sugar.

Cool to lukewarm.

Measure the very warm water into a large bowl.

Sprinkle or crumble in the yeast; stir until dissolved.

Add the lukewarm milk mixture, the eggs and about half of the flour; beat until smooth.

Add enough additional flour to make a soft dough.

Turn out onto a lightly floured board; knead until smooth and elastic, about 10 minutes.

Place in a greased bowl, turning to grease all sides.

Cover.

Let rise in a warm place, free from draft, until doubled in bulk, about 1 hour.

Punch down.

Turn out onto a lightly floured board; divide the dough in half.

Roll each half out into an 8-by-12-inch rectangle.

Press each rectangle of dough evenly into a well-greased pan, 13 by 9 by 2 inches.

Brush each cake lightly with melted butter or margarine; sprinkle each with 2 tablespoons sugar.

Peel, core and slice the apples.

Press the apple slices into the dough, sharp edges down and about ¼ inch apart.

Mix together 1 cup sugar and the cinnamon; sprinkle the top of each cake with half of the sugar mixture.

Cover.

Let rise in a warm place, free from draft, until doubled in bulk, about 45 minutes.

Bake in a hot oven (400° F.) for about 40 minutes.

Remove from the pans; cool on wire racks.

CHOCOLATE YEAST CAKE

(Makes 1 10-inch tube cake)

Preheat oven to 350° F., 20 minutes before cake is ready to bake.

¾ cup milk
2 packages or cakes yeast, dry or compressed
¼ cup very warm water
3 cups sifted flour
½ cup margarine or butter
2 cups sugar
3 eggs
6 ounces semi-sweet chocolate, melted
1 teaspoon baking soda
½ teaspoon salt
½ teaspoon vanilla

Scald the milk; cool to lukewarm.

Sprinkle or crumble the yeast into the very warm water in a small mixer bowl.

Stir until dissolved.

Add the milk and 1½ cups flour.

Beat at medium speed until smooth, about 30 seconds.

Cover; let rise in a warm place, free from draft, until light and spongy, about 30 minutes.

Meanwhile place the margarine or butter and sugar in a large mixer bowl.

Cream well at medium speed.

Add the eggs, one at a time, beating well after each addition.

Add the yeast mixture and remaining ingredients; beat until well blended, about 1 minute.

Turn into a well-greased 10-inch tube pan.

Cover; let rise in a warm place, free from draft, until light and bubbly, about 1 hour.

Bake in a moderate oven (350° F.) for about 50 minutes.

APPLE CRISP CAKE

(Makes 1 9-inch cake)

Preheat oven to 400° F., 20 minutes before cake is ready to bake.

⅓ cup milk
¼ cup sugar
6 tablespoons butter or margarine
¼ cup very warm water
1 package or cake yeast, dry or compressed
1 egg, well beaten
2½ cups sifted flour
3 tart green apples, peeled and sliced
½ cup brown sugar
1 teaspoon cinnamon
½ teaspoon nutmeg

Scald the milk; stir in the sugar and 2 tablespoons butter or margarine.

Cool to lukewarm.

Measure the very warm water into a large bowl.

Sprinkle or crumble in the yeast; stir until dissolved.

Add the lukewarm milk mixture, the egg and 2 cups flour.

Beat until smooth.

Spread the batter evenly in a well-greased 9-inch-square pan.

Arrange the apple slices on top.

Sprinkle with a combination of the brown sugar, remaining flour, cinnamon, nutmeg and remaining ¼ cup butter or margarine.

Cover; let rise in a warm place about 1 hour, free from draft, until doubled in bulk.

Bake in a hot oven (400° F.) for 30 minutes.

Serve warm, topped with vanilla ice cream.

COFFEE LACE

Preheat oven to 375° F., 20 minutes before lace is ready to bake.

For the batter
2 packages or cakes yeast, dry or compressed
⅓ cup very warm water
¾ cup sugar
2 teaspoons salt
1 cup butter or margarine
2 cups milk, scalded
7 cups sifted flour
2 eggs

To fill one braid
½ cup brown sugar
1 teaspoon cinnamon
½ cup apricot preserves
slivered almonds

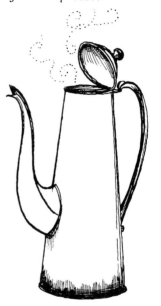

Dissolve the yeast in the very warm water.

In a mixing bowl combine the sugar, salt and butter or margarine.

Add the scalded milk.

Stir until the shortening melts.

Cool to lukewarm.

Add 4 cups flour to the lukewarm milk mixture and, with the electric mixer on medium speed, beat for 2 minutes.

Add the eggs and the yeast mixture.

With the electric mixer on medium speed, beat ½ minute.

With a spoon blend in the remaining 3 cups flour and beat until smooth, about 2 minutes.

The batter will be stiff.

Cover.

[74]

Let rise in a warm place, free from draft, until doubled in bulk, about 50 minutes.

Stir down and turn out onto a floured board.

Cover; let rest for 5 minutes.

For 1 braid, roll ⅓ of the dough into a 14-by-8-inch rectangle.

Brush generously with melted margarine or butter.

Place on a well-greased baking sheet.

Combine the brown sugar and cinnamon and sprinkle down the center of the rectangle in a strip 3 inches wide.

Top with the apricot preserves and almonds.

At each side of the filling make cuts 2 inches apart (2 inches into the dough), making 7 strips on each side.

Cross the strips over the filling.

Cover.

Let rise in a warm place, free from draft, until doubled in bulk, about 30 to 40 minutes.

Bake in a moderate oven (375° F.) until golden brown, 20 to 30 minutes.

Brush with Sugar Glaze (below).

If desired, repeat twice with the remaining dough or shape as desired into rolls or coffee cakes.

Sugar Glaze

1 tablespoon butter or margarine
3 tablespoons top milk
½ teaspoon lemon extract
confectioner's sugar

Melt 1 tablespoon margarine or butter.

Add 3 tablespoons top milk.

Heat but do not boil.

Add enough confectioner's sugar to make a thin creamy glaze.

Blend in ½ teaspoon lemon extract.

QUICK 'N' EASY COFFEE CAKE

(Makes 1 cake and 9 muffins)

Preheat oven to 400° F., 20 minutes before cake is ready to bake.

1 cup milk
⅔ cup granulated sugar
1½ teaspoons salt
8 tablespoons butter or margarine
½ cup warm water
2 packages or cakes yeast, dry or compressed
2 eggs
4 cups sifted white flour
½ cup brown sugar
¼ cup chopped nuts

Scald the milk.

Stir in the granulated sugar, the salt and 6 tablespoons butter or margarine.

Cool to lukewarm.

Measure into a bowl the warm (not hot) water.

(Cool to lukewarm for compressed yeast.)

Sprinkle or crumble in the yeast.

Stir until dissolved.

Add the lukewarm milk mixture.

Stir in the eggs, well beaten.

Stir in the flour.

Stir only enough to dampen the flour.

Fill well-greased muffin pans half full.

Pour the remaining batter into a well-greased 8-inch-square pan.

Mix together the brown sugar, 2 tablespoons butter or margarine, and the chopped nuts.

Sprinkle on top of the muffins and coffee cake.

Cover.

Let rise in a warm place, free from draft, until doubled in bulk, about 50 minutes.

Bake at 400° F. for about 20 to 25 minutes.

DUTCH APPLE CAKE
(Makes 1 9-inch cake)

Preheat oven to 400° F., 20 minutes before cake is ready to bake.

⅓ cup milk
¼ cup granulated sugar
½ teaspoon salt
4 tablespoons butter or margarine
¼ cup warm water
1 package or cake yeast, dry or compressed
1 egg
1⅓ cups sifted flour
1½ cups canned apple slices, drained
2 tablespoons brown sugar
¼ teaspoon cinnamon
¼ teaspoon nutmeg

Scald the milk.

Stir in the granulated sugar, the salt and 2 tablespoons butter or margarine.

Cool to lukewarm.

Measure into a bowl the warm (not hot) water.

(Cool to lukewarm for compressed yeast.)

Sprinkle or crumble in the yeast.

Stir until dissolved.

Stir in the lukewarm milk mixture.

Add the egg, well beaten, and the flour.

Beat until smooth.

Spread the dough evenly in a greased pan, 9 by 9 by 2 inches.

Arrange on top the canned apple slices.

Sprinkle with a mixture of the brown sugar, cinnamon and nutmeg.

Dot with 2 tablespoons butter or margarine.

Cover and let rise in a warm place, free from draft, until doubled in bulk, about 40 minutes.

Bake in a hot oven (400° F.) for 25 minutes.

CINNAMON APPLE LOAF

(Makes 2 loaves)

Preheat oven to 375° F., 20 minutes before loaves are ready to bake.

⅓ cup milk
⅓ cup sugar
¾ teaspoon salt
3 tablespoons butter or margarine
⅓ cup very warm water
1 package or cake yeast, dry or compressed
2 eggs
3½ cups sifted flour (about) or 3 cups
  unsifted flour (about)
melted butter or margarine
1 cup sugar
1 teaspoon cinnamon
½ teaspoon nutmeg
2 medium-to-large apples

Scald the milk; stir in ⅓ cup sugar, the salt and the butter or margarine.

Cool to lukewarm.

Measure the very warm water into a large bowl.

Sprinkle or crumble in the yeast; stir until dissolved.

Add the lukewarm milk mixture, eggs and half the flour; beat until smooth.

Add enough additional flour to make a soft dough.

Turn out onto a lightly floured board; knead until smooth and elastic, about 10 minutes.

Place in a greased bowl, turning to grease all sides.

Cover.

Let rise in a warm place, free from draft, until doubled in bulk, about 1 hour.

Punch down.

Turn out onto a lightly floured board; divide the dough in half.

Roll one half out into an 8-by-12-inch rectangle.

Brush lightly with melted butter or margarine.

Mix together the cinnamon, nutmeg and 1 cup sugar.

Sprinkle ⅓ of the sugar mixture on the dough.

Roll the dough up tightly from each 8-inch side toward the center to form a scroll-shaped loaf.

Make 7 slashes about 1 inch apart across both rolls of dough, going about halfway down into the dough.

Place the loaf in a well-greased bread pan, 9 by 5 by 3 inches.

Pare, core and slice 1 apple.

Press the apple slices, sharp edge down, into the slashes in the dough.

Brush lightly with melted butter or margarine.

Repeat with the remaining half of the dough and the other apple.

Sprinkle each loaf with half of the remaining sugar mixture.

Cover.

Let rise in a warm place, free from draft, until doubled in bulk, about 1 hour.

Bake in a moderate oven (375° F.) for about 35 minutes.

Serve warm.

APPLE CRUMB COFFEE CAKE
(Makes 1 9-inch cake)

Preheat oven to 375° F., 20 minutes before cake is ready to bake.

¼ cup very warm water
1 package or cake yeast, dry or compressed
½ cup (1 stick) margarine or butter,
    softened
½ cup sugar
½ teaspoon salt
3 eggs
¼ cup milk
2⅓ cups unsifted flour

Measure the very warm water into a small warm bowl.
Sprinkle or crumble in the yeast.
Stir until dissolved.
Cream the butter or margarine thoroughly in a large electric-mixer bowl.
Gradually add the sugar and salt.
Cream together.
Add the yeast mixture, eggs and milk.
Beat at medium speed until well blended.
Gradually add and blend in the flour while beating at medium speed; beat until the mixture is well blended.
Spread the batter in a well-greased pan, 9 by 9 by 2 inches.
Arrange Apple Crumb Topping (below) over the dough.
Cover and let rise in a warm place, free from draft, until doubled in bulk, about 1 hour.
Bake in a moderate oven (375° F.) for about 35 to 40 minutes.
Turn out of the pan and cool on a wire rack.

Apple Crumb Topping

2 or 3 large apples
⅔ cup sugar
½ cup flour
2 teaspoons cinnamon
6 tablespoons butter or margarine

Core, peel and slice the apples and arrange on the dough.
Combine the remaining ingredients and mix until crumbly.
Sprinkle over the apples.

SWEDISH CARDAMOM BRAID

(Makes 1 large braid)

Preheat oven to 350° F., 20 minutes before braid is ready to bake.

> ½ cup milk
> ½ cup sugar plus 2 tablespoons
> 1½ teaspoons salt
> ¼ cup butter or margarine
> ½ cup warm water
> 2 packages or cakes yeast, dry or compressed
> 2 eggs, beaten
> 5 cups sifted white flour
> 1½ teaspoons ground cardamom
> ½ cup seedless raisins
> 1 egg white

Scald the milk.

Stir in ½ cup sugar, the salt and the butter or margarine.
Cool to lukewarm.

Measure into a bowl the warm (not hot) water.

(Cool to lukewarm for compressed yeast.)

Sprinkle or crumble in the yeast.

Stir until dissolved.

Stir in the lukewarm milk mixture.

Add the beaten eggs, 3 cups flour, and the cardamom and raisins.

Beat until smooth.

Stir in an additional 2 cups sifted enriched flour (about).

Turn the dough out on a lightly floured board.

Knead until smooth and elastic.

Place in a greased bowl; brush the top with soft shortening. Cover.

Let rise in a warm place, free from draft, until doubled in bulk, about 1 hour.

Punch down and turn out on a lightly floured board.

Divide the dough into thirds.

Roll each part into a strand 10 inches long, tapering the ends.

Braid loosely.

Place on a greased baking sheet.

Cover.

Let rise in a warm place, free from draft, until doubled in bulk, about 1 hour.

Before baking, brush with the egg white and 2 tablespoons sugar.

Bake at 350° F. for about 35 minutes.

GOLDEN TWIST RINGS

PEANUT TWIST

CINNAMON CRESCENTS

Makes: 1 Golden Twist Ring
1 Peanut Twist
12 Cinnamon Crescents

Preheat oven to 400° F., 20 minutes before ready to bake.

Basic Dough

¾ cup milk
¼ cup sugar
1½ teaspoons salt
1 cup (2 sticks) butter or margarine
½ cup very warm water
2 packages or cakes yeast, dry or compressed
3 egg yolks, beaten
4½ cups sifted or 3½ cups unsifted
flour

Scald the milk; stir in ¼ cup sugar, the salt and the butter or margarine; cool to lukewarm.

Measure the very warm water into a large bowl.

Sprinkle or crumble in the yeast; stir until dissolved.

Add the lukewarm milk mixture and beaten egg yolks; stir to blend.

Add the flour and beat until well blended.

Cover tightly with aluminum foil.

Refrigerate at least 4 hours or overnight.

Golden Twist Rings

Divide the dough into 3 parts.

Divide ⅓ of the dough in half.

Roll each half into a strip 18 inches long.

Twist the 2 strips around each other.

Place on a greased baking sheet.

Form into a ring; tuck the end pieces under the ring and seal.

Cover; let rise in a warm place, free from draft, until doubled in bulk and light, about 1 hour.

Bake in a hot oven (400° F.) for about 15 minutes.

Cool.

Frost with Confectioner's-Sugar Icing (p. 63) and sprinkle with finely chopped nuts.

Peanut Twist

This takes ½ cup peanuts.

Knead ½ cup chopped peanuts into ⅓ of the dough and divide this dough in half.

Roll each half into a strip 18 inches long.

Twist the 2 strips around each other.

Place on a greased baking sheet.

Seal the ends of the twist and tuck under.

Cover; let rise in a warm place, free from draft, until doubled in bulk, about 1 hour.

Bake in a hot oven (400° F.) for about 20 minutes.

Cool.

Frost with Confectioner's-Sugar Icing (p. 63).

Cinnamon Crescents

This takes ½ cup sugar and 1 teaspoon cinnamon.

Roll the remaining ⅓ of the dough into a 12-inch circle.

Brush with melted butter or margarine.

Cut into 12 pie-shaped pieces.

Sprinkle with ¾ of a mixture of ½ cup sugar and 1 teaspoon cinnamon.

Beginning at the rounded edge, roll up.

Place on a greased baking sheet, with the point underneath. Curve in half circles.

Brush with melted butter or margarine.

Sprinkle with the remaining ¼ of the sugar-cinnamon mixture.

Bake in a hot oven (400° F.) for 12 to 15 minutes.

TO SHAPE ROLLS

Pan Rolls

Form the dough into small balls about 1 ounce each and set close together in a round pan.

Crescents

Roll a piece of dough into a 12-inch circle ¼ inch thick.
Cut into wedge-shaped pieces.
Brush with butter and roll up from the wide end.
Put on a baking sheet with the pointed end underneath.

Cloverleaf

Use muffin tins to bake these.
Make tiny balls of dough and put 3 into each buttered muffin cup.

Twists and Circles

Roll the dough to ¼-inch thickness.
Spread with butter.
Cut in ½-inch strips and twist the strips into circles or knots.

Parker House Rolls

Roll dough to ¼-inch thickness.
Cut into 1½-inch squares.
Brush well with soft butter and fold in half.
Place close together in a buttered pan.

AMBROSIA ROLLS

(Makes 28 rolls)

Preheat oven to 350° F., 20 minutes before rolls are ready to bake.

¾ cup milk
½ cup sugar
1½ teaspoons salt
½ cup (1 stick) butter or margarine
¾ cup very warm water
3 packages yeast, dry or compressed
2 eggs, beaten
6 cups sifted flour (about)
½ cup butter, melted
1½ cups brown sugar
grated rind of 2 oranges
1½ cups flaked coconut

Scald the milk; remove from heat.

Stir in ½ cup sugar, the salt and ½ cup butter or margarine; cool to lukewarm.

Measure the very warm water into a large bowl.

Sprinkle or crumble in the yeast; stir until dissolved.

Stir in the lukewarm milk mixture and eggs.

Add 3 cups flour; beat until smooth.

Stir in additional flour to make a soft dough.

Turn the dough out onto a floured board; knead until smooth and elastic, about 8 to 10 minutes, sprinkling additional flour on the board as needed to keep the dough from sticking.

Place the dough in a greased bowl twice the size of the dough; turn the dough to grease it on all sides.

Cover.

Let rise in a warm place, free from draft, until doubled in bulk, about 25 minutes.

Punch the dough down and turn it out on a lightly floured board.

Cut the dough in half.

Roll out each half into an oblong about 12 by 16 inches.

Brush each with half of the melted butter.

Mix the brown sugar, grated orange rind and coconut together; sprinkle half over each oblong.

Roll up from the long side, as for a jelly roll, to make a roll 16 inches long.

Seal the sides.

Cut into 14 equal pieces.

Place, cut side up, in 2 greased 9-inch layer-cake pans.

Cover.

Let rise in a warm place, free from draft, until doubled in bulk, about 20 minutes.

Bake in a moderate oven (350° F.) for about 30 minutes, or until done.

APRICOT PEANUT SQUARES

(Makes 24 squares)

Preheat oven to 350° F., 20 minutes before squares are ready to bake.

> *½ cup very warm water*
> *2 packages or cakes yeast, dry or compressed*
> *2 tablespoons sugar*
> *1 teaspoon salt*
> *¼ cup (½ stick) melted butter or*
>   *margarine*
> *2 eggs*
> *2 cups sifted flour or 1½ cups unsifted*
>   *flour*
> *¾ cup chopped cocktail peanuts*
> *1 cup apricot preserves*
> *¼ cup (½ stick) melted butter or*
>   *margarine*
> *1 teaspoon vanilla*

Measure the very warm water into a large bowl.

Sprinkle or crumble in the yeast; stir until dissolved.

Stir in the sugar, salt, ¼ cup melted butter or margarine, eggs and 1 cup flour.

Beat until smooth.

Add the balance of the flour.

Cover.

Let rise in a warm place, free from draft, until doubled in bulk, about 45 minutes.

Meanwhile mix together the cocktail peanuts, apricot preserves, ¼ cup melted butter or margarine and the vanilla.

Blend well.

When the batter has doubled in bulk, stir down.

Spread in a well-greased jelly-roll pan (10 by 15 inches).

Spread the apricot-peanut mixture over the batter.

Let rise in a warm place, free from draft, until doubled in bulk, about 25 minutes.

Bake in a moderate oven (350° F.) until done, about 30 to 35 minutes.

Turn out on a wire rack to cool.

Cut into squares to serve.

SHAPED BATTER ROLLS

(Makes 24 rolls)

Preheat oven to 400° F., 20 minutes before rolls are ready to bake.

> *¾ cup milk*
> *¼ cup sugar*
> *1 teaspoon salt*
> *¼ cup (½ stick) butter or margarine*
> *½ cup very warm water*
> *2 packages yeast, dry or compressed*
> *1 egg*
> *3½ cups* unsifted *flour (about)*

Scald the milk; stir in the sugar, salt and butter or margarine; cool to lukewarm.

Measure the very warm water into a large bowl.

Sprinkle or crumble in the yeast; stir until dissolved.

Add the lukewarm milk mixture, the egg and 2 cups unsifted flour; beat until smooth.

Stir in the remaining flour to make a soft dough.

Cover; let rise in a warm place, free from draft, until doubled in bulk, about 30 minutes.

Punch down.

Turn out onto a lightly floured board and shape into rolls of various shapes.

Cover; let rise in a warm place, free from draft, until doubled in bulk, about 30 minutes.

Bake in a hot oven (400° F.) for 15 minutes.

EASY REFRIGERATOR ROLLS

(Makes about 48 medium rolls)

Preheat oven to 400° F., 20 minutes before rolls are ready to bake.

2 packages or cakes yeast, dry or compressed
2 cups very warm water
½ cup sugar
2 teaspoons salt
¼ cup soft shortening or butter
1 egg
6½ to 7 cups sifted *flour*

In a mixing bowl, dissolve the yeast in the very warm water.
Stir in the remaining ingredients except the flour.
Mix in flour by hand until the dough is easy to handle.
Place in a greased bowl, turning once to grease the top.
Cover with a cloth; place in the refrigerator. (The dough keeps for about 5 days.)
About 2 hours before baking, shape the dough into the desired rolls and coffee cakes.
Cover and let rise until doubled in bulk (1½ to 2 hours).
Bake in a hot oven (400° F.) for 12 to 15 minutes.

ENGLISH BATH BUNS

(Makes 24 buns)

Preheat oven to 350° F., 20 minutes before buns are ready to bake.

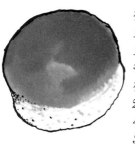

½ cup milk
1½ cups sugar
1 teaspoon salt
¾ cup (1½ sticks) butter or margarine
½ cup very warm water
2 packages or cakes yeast, dry or compressed
4 egg yolks
3 eggs
4½ cups sifted flour
½ teaspoon lemon extract
½ cup chopped candied fruit
¼ cup sliced blanched almonds

Scald the milk; stir in ½ cup sugar, the salt and butter or margarine.

Cool to lukewarm.

Measure the very warm water into a large bowl.

Sprinkle or crumble the yeast into the very warm water and stir until dissolved.

Add the lukewarm milk mixture, egg yolks, eggs, sifted flour and lemon extract.

Beat thoroughly until smooth, about 5 minutes.

Cover and let rise in a warm place, free from draft, until doubled in bulk, about 1¼ hours.

Stir down, cover well and chill in the refrigerator overnight.

Divide into small pieces; shape into balls and place on greased baking sheets.

Cover and let rise in a warm place, free from draft, until doubled in bulk, about 50 minutes.

Before baking, press candied fruit and almonds into the tops.

Brush with an egg mixed with milk.

Sprinkle the remaining 1 cup sugar over the tops.

Bake in a moderate oven (350° F.) for 15 to 20 minutes.

Remove from the baking sheets and serve warm.

HERB BREAD STICKS

(Makes 24 sticks)

Preheat oven to 400° F., 20 minutes before sticks are ready to bake.

> *1¼ cups warm (not hot) water*
> *1 package or cake yeast, dry or compressed*
> *3 tablespoons sugar*
> *1½ teaspoons salt*
> *1 tablespoon margarine or butter*
> *3½ cups sifted flour (about)*
> *3 teaspoons caraway seeds*
> *1 teaspoon sage*

Measure the water into a large bowl (warm, not hot, water for active dry yeast; lukewarm water for compressed yeast).

Sprinkle or crumble in the yeast.

Stir until dissolved.

Add the sugar, salt and margarine or butter.

Add and stir in 2 teaspoons caraway seeds, the sage and the flour.

Turn the dough out on a lightly floured board; knead until smooth and elastic, about 10 minutes.

Place in a greased bowl, turning once to grease the top.

Cover; let rise in a warm place, free from draft, until doubled in bulk, about 1 hour.

Punch down, turn out on a floured board and cut into 2 equal portions.

Roll each half into a roll 12 inches long; cut each into 12 even pieces.

Roll each piece on the board with the palms of your hands to form a rope about ⅓ inch thick and 12 inches long.

Place the sticks on a greased baking sheet.

Sprinkle lightly with the remaining caraway seeds.

Cover.

Let rise in a warm place, free from draft, until doubled, about 1 hour.

Bake in a hot oven (400° F.) for 15 to 20 minutes.

LIGHT ROLLS

(Makes about 36 rolls)

Preheat oven to 400° F., 20 minutes before rolls are ready to bake.

> 2 *cups milk*
> ½ *cup sugar*
> 2 *teaspoons salt*
> ½ *cup shortening or butter*
> 2 *packages dry yeast*
> ¼ *cup warm water*
> 1 *egg*
> 1 *teaspoon baking powder*
> ¼ *teaspoon soda*
> 7 *to 8 cups sifted flour*

Scald the milk.

Stir in the sugar, salt and shortening or butter.

Cool to lukewarm.

Dissolve the yeast in the warm (not hot) water.

Stir in the egg.

Add the lukewarm milk mixture, baking powder, soda and half the flour.

Beat until smooth.

Stir in enough remaining flour to make a soft dough.

Beat hard for several minutes.

Cover and let rise in a warm place, free from draft, until doubled in bulk, about 1 hour.

Punch down and shape into rolls of various shapes.

Cover and let rise again until doubled in bulk, about 30 to 45 minutes.

Bake in a hot oven (400° F.) for 15 minutes.

[*94*]

SAFFRON BUNS
(Makes 16 buns)

Preheat oven to 375° F., 20 minutes before buns are ready to bake.

> ¾ cup milk
> ⅓ cup sugar
> 1 teaspoon salt
> ¼ cup (½ stick) margarine or butter
> 1 teaspoon saffron
> 2 tablespoons boiling water
> ½ cup very warm water
> 2 packages or cakes yeast, dry or compressed
> 1 egg, beaten
> 4 cups sifted flour (about)
> ¼ cup currants or seedless raisins

Scald the milk; stir in the sugar, salt and margarine; cool to lukewarm.

Meanwhile add the saffron to the boiling water; let stand.

Measure the very warm water into a large bowl.

Sprinkle or crumble in the yeast; stir until dissolved.

Stir in the lukewarm milk mixture, beaten egg, saffron and 2 cups flour; beat until smooth.

Stir in the currants, then enough remaining flour to make a soft dough.

Turn out onto a floured surface; knead until smooth and elastic, about 8 minutes.

Place in a greased bowl, turning to grease all sides.

Cover; let rise in a warm place, free from draft, until doubled in bulk, about 1 hour.

Punch down; turn out onto a floured board; cover and let rest for 10 minutes.

Cut off a piece of dough about 2 inches in diameter.

Divide the rest of the dough into 16 equal pieces.

Shape each piece into a ball; place in a well-greased small brioche mold or muffin cup.

Divide the 2-inch piece of dough into 16 pieces; shape each into a small ball.

Make a deep indentation in each bun; press a small ball into each indentation.

Cover; let rise in a warm place, free from draft, until doubled in bulk, about 30 minutes.

Bake in a moderate oven (375° F.) for about 15 minutes, or until done.

REFRIGERATOR WHOLE-WHEAT ROLLS
(Makes 48 rolls)

Preheat oven to 375° F., or as required, 20 minutes before rolls are ready to bake.

> *1 cup hot water*
> *⅔ cup sugar*
> *1 tablespoon salt*
> *¼ cup (½ stick) margarine or butter*
> *1 cup very warm water*
> *2 packages or cakes yeast, dry or compressed*
> *2 eggs, beaten*
> *1 cup whole-wheat flour*
> *6 cups sifted flour (about)*

Combine the hot water with the sugar, salt and margarine or butter; cool to lukewarm.

Measure the very warm water into a large bowl.

Sprinkle or crumble in the yeast; stir until dissolved.

Stir in the lukewarm mixture, beaten eggs, whole-wheat flour and 3 cups sifted flour; beat until smooth.

Stir in enough remaining flour to make a soft dough; mix well.

Place in a greased bowl, turning to grease all sides of the dough.

Cover closely with waxed paper or aluminum foil.

Store in the refrigerator until needed.

To use, punch the dough down and cut off the amount needed.

The dough may be kept 4 days in the refrigerator.

Strip Rolls

Use ¼ of the dough.

Roll out on a floured board to make an oblong 10 by 5 inches.

Let rest for 5 minutes.

Meanwhile melt 2 tablespoons margarine or butter in a 10-by-6-inch pan.

Cut the dough into 8 strips 5 inches long.

Dip each strip into melted margarine or butter, coating all sides.

Arrange the strips in a baking pan.

Cover; let rise in a warm place, free from draft, until doubled in bulk, about 1 hour.

Bake in a moderate oven (375° F.) for about 30 minutes, or until done.

Makes 8.

Pan Ring

Use ¼ of the dough.

On a floured board, roll out to make a 12-inch roll.

Cut into 12 equal pieces.

Shape each piece into a ball; roll in melted margarine or butter.

Place in a 9-inch greased ring mold.

Cover; let rise in a warm place, free from draft, until doubled in bulk, about 1 hour.

Bake in a moderate oven (375° F.) for about 30 minutes.

Makes 12.

Figure 8's

Use ¼ of the dough.

Roll out to ¼-inch thickness.

Cut with a doughnut cutter.

Twist once to make a figure 8.

Place on a greased baking sheet about 2 inches apart.

Cover; let rise in a warm place, free from draft, until doubled in bulk, about 1 hour.

Bake in a hot oven (400° F.) for about 12 to 15 minutes, or until done.

Makes 12.

Whole-Wheat English Muffins

Roll ¼ of the dough out to ¼-inch thickness.

Cut into 3-inch squares or rounds and place on a greased baking sheet.

Cover; let rise in a warm place, free from draft, until doubled in bulk, about 1 hour.

Bake on an ungreased griddle over low heat for about 10 minutes; turn and bake 10 minutes longer.

Or bake in an electric skillet with the temperature control at 325° F.

To serve, split and toast under the broiler.

Makes 12.

RAISED CORN ROLLS

(Makes 30–36 rolls)

Preheat oven to 400° F., 20 minutes before rolls are ready to bake.

½ cup yellow cornmeal
2 tablespoons sugar
1 teaspoon salt
2 tablespoons margarine or butter
¾ cup boiling water
¼ cup very warm water
1 package or cake yeast, dry or compressed
1 egg, beaten
3 cups sifted flour (about)

Combine the cornmeal, sugar and salt in a large bowl.
Add the margarine or butter.
Pour in the boiling water, stirring.
Cool to lukewarm.
Measure the very warm water into a small bowl.
Sprinkle or crumble in the yeast; stir until dissolved.
Stir yeast into the lukewarm cornmeal mixture; stir in the egg and 2 cups flour; beat until smooth.
Stir in remaining flour to make a soft dough.
Turn out onto a floured board; knead until smooth and elastic, about 10 minutes.
Place in a greased bowl, turning to grease all sides.
Cover; let rise in a warm place, free from draft, until doubled in bulk, about 1 hour.
Punch the dough down.
Turn out on a lightly floured board.
Divide the dough in half.
Cut each half into 9 to 12 equal parts and shape each into a ball.
Place about 3 inches apart on a greased baking sheet and pat to form a round of dough about ¾ inch thick.
Brush lightly with melted margarine or butter.
Cover; let rise in a warm place, free from draft, until doubled in bulk, about 1 hour.
Bake in a hot oven (400° F.) for about 20 minutes.

RICH GOLDEN ROLLS

(Makes 32 rolls)

Preheat oven to 400° F., 20 minutes before rolls are ready to bake.

½ cup milk
⅓ cup sugar
1 teaspoon salt
1 cup (2 sticks) margarine or butter
3 packages yeast, dry or compressed
½ cup warm (not hot) water
2 eggs
4¼ cups sifted flour (about)

Scald the milk; add the sugar, salt and margarine or butter. Cool to lukewarm.

In a large bowl dissolve the yeast in water (warm, not hot, water for dry yeast, lukewarm water for compressed yeast).

Add the lukewarm milk mixture, eggs and half the flour; beat until smooth.

Stir in enough remaining flour to make a soft dough.

Turn out onto a lightly floured board; knead until smooth and elastic, about 10 minutes.

Place in a greased bowl; brush the top with soft shortening.

Cover; let rise in a warm place, free from draft, until doubled in bulk, about 1 hour.

Punch down; divide into quarters.

Roll each quarter out on a lightly floured board to make a circle ⅛ inch thick; cut the circle into 8 wedges.

Roll up each wedge, starting at the wide end.

Place the rolls, with the point underneath, on a lightly greased cookie sheet; if desired, turn the ends in to make crescent shapes.

Cover; let rise in a warm place, free from draft, until doubled in bulk, about 1 hour.

Bake in a hot oven (400° F.) for about 20 minutes, or until golden.

SUNDAY BREAKFAST ROLLS

(Makes 36 rolls)

Preheat oven to 400° F., 20 minutes before rolls are ready to bake.

4 cups sifted flour
¼ cup sugar
1 teaspoon salt
1 teaspoon grated lemon rind
1 cup (2 sticks) margarine or butter
1 package or cake yeast, dry or compressed
¼ cup very warm water
1 cup milk, lukewarm
2 eggs, beaten
1 cup sugar
1 tablespoon cinnamon

In a large bowl, combine the flour, ¼ cup sugar, the salt and grated lemon rind.

With a pastry blender or 2 knives cut the shortening into the flour mixture.

Sprinkle or crumble the yeast into the very warm water; stir until dissolved.

Scald the milk and cool to lukewarm.

Add the dissolved yeast, lukewarm milk and eggs to the flour mixture.

Toss lightly until thoroughly combined.

Cover tightly and refrigerate overnight.

Divide the dough in half.

Roll half on a well-floured board into a rectangle 18 by 12 inches.

Sprinkle with half the mixture of 1 cup sugar and the cinnamon.

Roll up tightly, beginning at the wide side.

Cut each roll into 1-inch slices.

Place, cut side up, on a greased baking sheet.

Flatten with the palm of your hand.

Repeat with the remaining dough and sugar-cinnamon mixture.

Bake immediately in a hot oven (400° F.) for about 12 minutes.

APPLE DANISH

(Makes 24 pastries)

Preheat oven to 375° F., 20 minutes before pastries are ready to bake.

¾ cup milk
⅓ cup sugar
2 teaspoons salt
⅓ cup butter or margarine
2 packages or cakes yeast, dry or compressed
¼ cup warm (not hot) water (cool to
 lukewarm for compressed yeast)
½ teaspoon lemon extract
3 eggs, beaten
4½ cups sifted flour
1 cup (2 sticks) butter or margarine
1 no. 2 can (2½ cups) sliced apples
1 cup sugar mixed with 2 tablespoons
 cinnamon

Scald the milk; stir in the sugar, salt and ⅓ cup butter or margarine.

Cool to lukewarm.

In a large bowl dissolve the yeast in warm water.

Add the lukewarm milk mixture.

Stir in the lemon extract and eggs.

Add the flour gradually.

Place the dough in a greased 9-by-13-inch pan.

Chill in the refrigerator for 1 to 2 hours.

Turn the chilled dough out onto a floured. board.

Roll into a rectangle 12 by 16 inches.

Spread ⅓ cup butter or margarine over ⅔ of the dough.

Fold the unspread portion of the dough over half the covered portion.

Fold the third section over the first two.

Roll the dough to its original size and repeat this process twice, using the remaining butter or margarine.

Return the dough to the refrigerator and chill overnight.

When ready to make, divide the dough in half.

Roll into a rectangle 14 by 9 inches.

Cut into strips 14 by ¾ inches.

Twist and form each strip into a special roll, building up the sides.

Fill the shells with drained apple slices.

Sprinkle with the cinnamon-sugar combination.

Cover.

Let rise in a warm place, free from draft, until doubled in bulk.

Bake in a moderate oven (375° F.) for about 12 minutes.

CHEESE CRESCENTS
(Makes 24 crescents)

Preheat oven to 400° F., 20 minutes before crescents are ready to bake.

1¼ cups milk
2½ tablespoons sugar
1½ teaspoons salt
¼ cup butter or margarine
¼ cup warm water
1 package or cake yeast, dry or compressed
4¼ cups sifted white flour (about)
1 cup Cheddar cheese, grated

Scald the milk.
Add and stir the sugar, salt and butter or margarine.
Cool to lukewarm.
Measure into a bowl the warm (not hot) water.
(Cool to lukewarm for compressed yeast.)
Sprinkle or crumble in the yeast.
Stir until dissolved.
Add the lukewarm milk mixture.
Add the flour.
Add and stir in the cheese.
Turn the dough out on a lightly floured board; divide into 3 equal pieces.
Roll out each piece into a circle about 9½ inches in diameter and ¼ inch thick.
Cut with a sharp knife into 8 pie-shaped pieces.
Brush lightly with melted margarine or butter.
Roll up, beginning at the wide end, and seal ends firmly.
Place on a greased baking sheet about 2 inches apart.
Curve in half-circles.
Cover with a clean damp towel.
Let rise in a warm place, free from draft, until doubled in bulk, about 45 minutes.
Bake at 400° F. for about 15 minutes.

BRIOCHE

(Makes 24 individual brioches)

Preheat oven to 375° F., 20 minutes before brioches are ready to bake.

½ cup milk
½ cup (1 stick) butter or margarine
⅓ cup sugar
1 teaspoon salt
¼ cup very warm water
1 package or cake yeast, dry or compressed
3 whole eggs
1 egg yolk
3½ cups unsifted flour or
*   4 cups sifted flour*
1 egg white
1 tablespoon sugar

Scald the milk; cool to lukewarm.

Cream the butter or margarine in a large bowl.

Gradually add ⅓ cup sugar and the salt, and cream together.

Measure the very warm water into a small bowl; sprinkle or crumble in the yeast; stir until dissolved.

Add the dissolved yeast and lukewarm milk to the creamed mixture; then add the eggs, egg yolk and flour.

Beat vigorously for 2 minutes.

Cover.

Let rise in a warm place, free from draft, until more than doubled in bulk, about 2 hours.

Stir down and beat vigorously for 2 minutes.

Cover tightly with aluminum foil and refrigerate overnight.

Beat down; turn the soft dough out onto a lightly floured board.

Divide into 2 pieces, one about ¾ the weight of the dough and the other about ¼ the weight of the dough.

Cut the larger piece into 24 equal pieces.

[*105*]

Form into smooth balls.

Place in well-greased muffin pans, 2¾ by 1¼ inches.

Cut the smaller piece into 24 equal pieces.

Form into smooth balls.

Make a deep indentation in the center of each large ball; dampen slightly with cold water.

Press a small ball into each indentation.

Let rise in a warm place, free from draft, until doubled in bulk, about 50 minutes.

Brush with a mixture of 1 egg white and 1 tablespoon sugar.

Bake in a moderate oven (375° F.) for about 15 to 20 minutes.

QUICK CELERY CRESCENTS
(Makes 12 crescents)

Preheat oven to 425° F., 20 minutes before crescents are ready to bake.

> ½ cup milk
> 2 tablespoons sugar
> 1½ teaspoons salt
> 1 cake yeast or 1 package
>   dry yeast
> ½ cup lukewarm water
> 3 cups sifted flour
> 3 tablespoons melted shortening
>   or butter
> ½ teaspoon salt
> 1 teaspoon celery seeds

Scald the milk, add the sugar and 1½ teaspoons salt; cool to lukewarm.

Dissolve the yeast in the lukewarm water and add to the lukewarm milk.

Add 1½ cups flour and beat until perfectly smooth.

Add the melted shortening and remaining flour, or enough to make an easily handled dough, and knead well.

Roll the dough into a circular shape about ¼ inch thick.

Cut into 12 pie-shaped pieces.

Brush lightly with melted butter or margarine and, beginning at the wide end, roll up to the pointed end.

Shape into crescents and place on a well-greased baking sheet with the pointed end underneath.

Brush with melted butter or margarine; sprinkle with ½ teaspoon salt and the celery seeds.

Cover and set in a warm place, free from draft.

Let rise until light, about 1 hour.

Bake in a hot oven (425° F.) for 20 minutes.

CHOCOLATE STICKY BUNS
(Makes 18 buns)

Preheat oven to 350° F., 20 minutes before buns are ready to bake.

For the batter
1 package or cake yeast, dry or compressed
⅓ cup very warm water (105° F.)
⅓ cup sugar
1 teaspoon salt
½ cup (1 stick) butter or margarine
¾ cup milk, scalded
3½ cups sifted flour
1 egg

For the topping
½ cup (1 stick) margarine or butter
1 cup brown sugar
¼ cup corn syrup
3 tablespoons cocoa
1 cup whole pecans

For the filling
1 cup sugar
2 tablespoons cocoa
2 teaspoons cinnamon

In a small bowl, dissolve the yeast in the very warm water.

In a mixing bowl, combine the sugar, salt and butter or margarine.

Add the scalded milk.

Stir until the shortening melts.

Cool to lukewarm.

Add 1½ cups flour to the lukewarm milk mixture.

Blend with an electric mixer at medium speed; beat for 2 minutes.

Add the egg and the yeast mixture.

Beat at medium speed for ½ minute.

With a spoon, blend in the remaining 2 cups flour and beat until smooth, about 2 minutes.

The batter will be stiff.

Cover.

Let rise in a warm place, free from draft, until doubled in bulk, about 50 minutes.

Meanwhile prepare the topping.

In a saucepan melt ½ cup butter or margarine; add the brown sugar, corn syrup and cocoa.

Bring to a boil and cook for 1 minute.

Divide the syrup into 2 9-inch cake pans.

Arrange the pecans in the syrup.

When the batter has doubled, stir down and turn out onto a well-floured board.

Cover; let rest for 5 minutes.

Divide the dough in half.

Roll out 1 piece of dough into an oblong about 14 by 9 inches.

Brush lightly with melted margarine or butter.

Combine 1 cup sugar and the cocoa and cinnamon for the filling.

Sprinkle the oblong with half of the sugar filling.

Roll up as for a jelly roll to make a roll 9 inches long.

Seal the edges firmly.

Cut into 9 equal pieces.

Place in the prepared 9-inch cake pan.

Repeat with the remaining dough.

Cover.

Let rise in a warm place, free from draft, until doubled in bulk, about 1 hour.

Bake in a moderate oven (350° F.) for 35 minutes.

Turn out of the pan immediately.

Irish Soda Bread is the popular brown bread in Irish country homes, although sliced white bread now appears in gay waxed-paper wrappers in Dublin and other towns.

The whole-wheat flour is stone ground, and baking soda, cream of tartar and sour milk are used to lighten it.

Every farmer's wife had to make butter almost every day, for it was one of the main cash crops. There was always buttermilk from the churning, and it was the family drink and handy for the baking.

The soda is alkali and the cream of tartar acid. When they are mixed with sour milk or buttermilk, gas is formed and the heat of the oven makes the gas bubbles expand in a way similar to the action of yeast.

Sometimes soda bread is made of all whole wheat and sometimes with part whole wheat and part white.

Sweet milk can be soured by taking two tablespoons of milk out of a full cup and substituting two tablespoons of vinegar or lemon juice. Let this mixture stand about ten minutes before you use it.

BASIC WHOLE-MEAL IRISH SODA BREAD
(Makes 1 large loaf)

Preheat oven to 400° F.

> ½ cup sifted white flour
> 1½ cups whole wheat flour—not sifted
> 1 teaspoon salt
> 1 teaspoon baking soda
> ½ teaspoon cream of tartar
> 1 teaspoon granulated sugar
> ¾ cup sour milk or buttermilk

In a bowl mix together all the dry ingredients by stirring and tossing with a spoon or fork. Make a hole in the center, pour in the sour milk or buttermilk and mix together to a dough. If a little too dry, add a bit more milk so that you have a nice pliable dough.

Knead about ten times; form into a circular loaf; cut a deep cross on the top surface and bake for 50 minutes to one hour in a 400 degree oven.

This bread is best served the day it is baked as it is apt to dry out rather quickly. However, it can be sliced and toasted on the second day.

MAGGIE MURPHY'S POT OVEN BREAD

Down yonder in one of our big fields is a lovely mysterious ruin of an old house and grist mill—moss-covered stone walls, roof fallen in over a perfectly arched stone doorway—and at one end of this relic of the past is a tiny two-room cottage that was once the miller's cottage. There, almost fourscore years ago, Maggie Murphy first saw the light of day, and there she will live out all the days that are left to her.

Spry as a cricket, she bicycles the five miles into the village once a week and peddles back (uphill most of the way) with whole-wheat flour among her purchases.

She cooks over an open hearth fire and mixes her soda bread just as I gave you the recipe, but she has no oven—just a three-

legged iron pot oven. She sets this right in the red-hot coals on her hearth, rubs it inside with a bit of fat pork, drops her cake of whole-wheat dough into it, puts on the cover and then shovels some of the red coals onto the cover. Heat top and bottom she then has, and the bread bakes for an hour while she sits by the hearth, from time to time turning the handle on her wheel bellows—which makes a draft of air come up through the tiny hole under the coals, bringing them to life with a golden glow.

At just the right minute she brushes the hot coals off the cover, lowers the crane to catch the handle of the pot and swings it out away from the fire.

Out comes a perfectly baked, crusty loaf, fragrant and golden "and good enough for the likes of me," says my dear friend Maggie Murphy.

WHITE SODA BREAD
(Makes 1 loaf)

Preheat oven to 450° F.

> *1 pound white flour*
> *1 teaspoon salt*
> *1 teaspoon sugar*
> *2 teaspoons baking soda*
> *1 cup buttermilk or sour milk (about)*

Sift the dry ingredients several times through your fingers.
Add the milk gradually, mixing well.
Have the dough not too dry.
Turn it out onto a floured bread board and knead lightly just a few times.
Shape into a round flat loaf and cut a deep cross from side to side.
Bake on a flat pan in a hot oven (450° F.) for 45 minutes.

RAISIN SODA BREAD

(Makes 1 loaf)

Preheat oven to 450° F.
Use the White Soda Bread dough recipe (p. 112) and add

½ cup sugar
1 beaten egg
4 tablespoons butter, melted
½ cup seedless raisins
(or more), if you like raisins

GRIDDLE BREAD

Mix the White Soda Bread dough (p. 112).
Roll it out to about ¾ inch thick.

Cut in pieces any size you want and bake on a hot greased griddle for about 10 minutes on each side.

Eat while hot, with butter and honey on it.

PAN-FRIED SODA BREAD

Soda bread should be eaten the day it is made, for it dries out very quickly.

But when you have some left over, use it with bacon and eggs.

Fry some bacon and remove the bacon to drain off.

Into the hot bacon fat put slices of the soda bread and brown them on both sides.

Serve with a fried egg on top and the bacon on the side.

BARMBRACK

(Makes 2 loaves)

Preheat oven to 375° F.

¾ cup milk
½ cup sugar
1½ teaspoons salt
¼ cup margarine or butter
3 packages or cakes yeast,
*   dry or compressed*
½ cup very warm water
2 eggs, beaten
5 cups sifted flour (about)
grated rind of 1 lemon
1¼ cups golden seedless raisins
⅓ cup chopped mixed candied fruits

Scald the milk.

Stir in the sugar, salt and margarine or butter.

Cool to lukewarm.

Sprinkle or crumble the yeast into the very warm water in a large bowl.

Stir until dissolved.

Add the lukewarm milk mixture, beaten eggs and 3 cups flour.

Beat on the medium speed of the mixer for 2 minutes (or 300 vigorous strokes by hand).

Stir in the lemon rind and enough remaining flour to make a soft dough.

Turn the dough out onto a lightly floured board.

Knead until smooth and elastic.

Place in a greased bowl; brush the top with soft shortening. Cover.

Let rise in a warm place, free from draft, for about 40 minutes.

Punch down and turn out onto a lightly floured board.

Knead in the raisins and mixed candied fruit.

Divide in half.

[*114*]

Shape into loaves.

Place in 2 greased loaf pans, 9 by 5 by 3 inches.

Cover.

Let rise in a warm place, free from draft, until doubled in bulk, about 50 minutes.

Bake in a moderate oven (375° F.) for 30 to 35 minutes.

CAKE

There's only one way to make good homemade cake, and that is to measure everything exactly.

Use cake flour and double-acting baking powder. I prefer to sift my flour once before measuring it.

Use level measurements for everything, leveling off spoons or cups with a spatula.

Get your pans ready before you start mixing. Butter the pan, then sprinkle with flour and tip the pan back and forth until the flour coats the pan evenly. Then shake off the surplus flour.

Do not butter angel-food or sponge-cake pans except on the bottom.

Be sure your oven is the correct temperature. Check it with an oven thermometer.

Cooling cakes perfectly is very important. When you turn out a layer of cake onto a rack, it will be upside down. Don't leave it that way. Turn it and let it cool resting on the bottom flat side.

Sponge cakes and angel cakes can be cooled in the pan by turning the pan upside down on a cake rack for 1 hour. Then loosen the sides gently by running a knife or spatula around the side of the cake and around the center tube. It should slide out easily.

TWO-LAYER CAKE

Preheat oven to 375° F.

Butter and flour 2 9-inch layer-cake pans.

> *2 cups sifted cake flour*
> *2 teaspoons double-acting baking powder*
> *½ teaspoon salt*
> *½ cup butter (¼ pound)*
> *1 cup sugar*
> *3 eggs*
> *½ cup milk*
> *1 teaspoon vanilla*

Sift the flour once and measure.

Add the baking powder and salt and sift together.

Cream the butter and sugar in your electric mixer until soft and fluffy.

Separate the eggs and add the yolks to the butter and sugar, one at a time, beating well.

Remove the bowl from the mixer and add the flour and milk alternately by hand. This is best because overbeating after the flour is added makes a less tender cake.

Add the vanilla and mix well.

Beat the egg whites till stiff and place them on top of the batter.

Then carefully fold them into the batter, lifting it from the bottom up over and over. Do not beat or stir, just fold over and under.

Spoon evenly into the pans.

Bake at 375° F. for 25 minutes, or until brown and shrunken a little from the sides of the pan.

Turn out onto cake racks and immediately turn right side up by putting another cake rack on top and reversing them.

Let cool thoroughly.

DEVIL'S-FOOD CAKE

Preheat oven to 350° F.
Butter and flour 2 9-inch layer-cake pans.

¼ pound butter, very soft
2 cups sifted cake flour
¾ teaspoon salt
1 teaspoon baking soda
1¼ cups sugar
3 squares unsweetened chocolate, melted
1 teaspoon vanilla
¾ cup milk
2 eggs

Put the soft butter into a mixing bowl.
Put the sifted flour, salt, soda and sugar into a sifter and sift them right over the butter.
Add the milk and beat for 2 minutes.
Add the vanilla, melted chocolate and whole eggs.
Beat 1 minute.
Pour evenly into the pans.
Bake in a 350° F. oven for 25 minutes, or until slightly shrunken from the sides of the pan.
Turn out onto cake racks and immediately turn right side up.
Let cool thoroughly.
Ice with Seven-Minute Vanilla Frosting (p. 120).

OLD-FASHIONED CHOCOLATE FROSTING

1 cup sugar
4 level tablespoons cake flour
4 ounces unsweetened chocolate, cut into small bits
1½ cups milk
2 tablespoons butter

Put all the dry ingredients in a saucepan.
Mix well and add the milk.

Cook until it boils, stirring constantly, until thick and smooth.
Remove from the heat and add the butter, stirring well.
Cool and use to cover layers.

COCONUT LAYER CAKE

Make a Two-Layer Cake (p. 116).

Seven-Minute Coconut Frosting
2 egg whites, unbeaten
1½ cups fine granulated sugar
5 tablespoons water
1 teaspoon vanilla
1 can moist coconut

Put all the ingredients except the coconut and vanilla in the
top of a double boiler and mix well.

Place over boiling water and beat with a rotary egg beater or
electric hand beater for 7 minutes, no more, no less.

The frosting should be shiny and thick.

Remove from the heat.

Add the vanilla and beat a few turns more.

Spread one layer of cake with frosting and sprinkle with
some of the coconut.

Cover the top layer and sides with frosting and sprinkle the
rest of the coconut all over.

CHOCOLATE LAYER CAKE

Make a Two-Layer Cake (p. 116).

When the cake layers are cool, frost with Old-fashioned
Chocolate Frosting (p. 117).

CHOCOLATE ICEBOX CAKE

(Serves 8)

2 3½-ounce packages ladyfingers (24 double ones)
2 4-ounce packages sweet chocolate
12 tablespoons sweet butter (1½ bars) plus 1 extra
    tablespoon
3 eggs
¾ cup powdered sugar
3 tablespoons warm water
¼ cup granulated sugar
¼ cup water
¼ cup light rum

Butter a 2-quart straight-sided soufflé dish with 1 tablespoon butter.

Moisten the granulated sugar with ¼ cup water and boil for 5 minutes.

Remove from the fire and add the rum.

Cool partially.

Dip the ladyfingers quickly in and out of the syrup and stand them around the inside of the soufflé dish.

Lay 2 or 3 over the bottom.

Now melt the chocolate in 3 tablespoons warm water over hot (not boiling) water, stirring until smooth.

Stir in gradually the powdered sugar.

Separate the egg yolks from the whites.

Add the yolks, one at a time, beating well with a spoon.

Last of all, add 1½ bars sweet butter, a tablespoon at a time, being careful not to allow the water in the bottom of the double boiler to actually boil.

When all has been well blended, remove the top of the double boiler from the bottom.

Beat the egg whites until stiff but not dry, and fold them into the chocolate mixture.

When all the whites have disappeared, pour the whole into the ladyfinger-lined dish.

Cover and refrigerate overnight.

When ready to serve, turn out carefully onto a serving platter and send to the table.

SEVEN-MINUTE VANILLA FROSTING

1 egg white, unbeaten
⅔ cup fine granulated sugar
¼ teaspoon cream of tartar
2 tablespoons cold water
½ teaspoon vanilla

Put all the ingredients except the vanilla in the top of a double boiler.

Stir well until the sugar is dissolved.

Place over boiling water, but do not let the bottom of the top pot touch the water.

Beat with a rotary egg beater for about 7 minutes, beating continuously until the frosting is thick.

Remove from the heat and add the vanilla.

BROWN-SUGAR FROSTING

Use the recipe for Seven-Minute Vanilla Frosting (above), but substitute sifted light brown sugar for the white sugar.

CREAM CHEESE FROSTING

(Makes enough to top 2 8-inch layers)

Blend a 3-ounce package cream cheese with 1 tablespoon milk.

Gradually add 2½ cups sifted confectioner's sugar; blend well.

Mix in ½ teaspoon vanilla extract, if desired.

GATO-ALMOND CAKE (SPANISH)

(Serves 8)

Preheat oven to 325° F.

2 4½-ounce cans blanched almonds
6 eggs (separated)
grated rind of 1 lemon
½ teaspoon powdered cinnamon
1 cup granulated sugar
½ box vanilla cookies
5 tablespoons butter
confectioner's sugar in which you have kept a vanilla bean

Butter a round 9-inch cake tin with straight sides, using 1 tablespoon butter.

Grind or roll out a generous half-box of plain vanilla cookies and add to them 4 tablespoons melted butter.

Mix with a fork and line the sides and bottom of the pan, spreading the crumbs evenly. This takes a bit of patience.

Grind through a meat grinder, using the smallest cutter, the blanched almonds.

Separate the egg yolks from the whites.

Grate the rind of 1 lemon and add to the yolks.

Also add the cinnamon and granulated sugar.

Stir well with a wooden spoon until thoroughly mixed.

Add the ground almonds and stir well.

Beat the egg whites until stiff but not dry.

Stir these into the yolk-and-almond mixture.

Place evenly in the crumb-lined cake pan and bake in a 300°– 325° F. oven for about ½ hour.

The mixture should be set but still soft, not dry.

Cool a bit, run a knife around the edge, and turn out carefully onto a large round serving platter.

Sift copiously with confectioner's sugar.

Serve cold, with hot black coffee.

CHEESE CAKE

Preheat oven to 450° F.

Make 1 recipe Plain Pastry (p. 133) or Graham-Cracker Crust (p. 135).

1½ pounds dry cottage cheese
1 cup sour cream
½ cup sugar
2 tablespoons cornstarch
¼ teaspoon salt
2 eggs, separated
cinnamon sugar

Line a 9-inch pie pan with plain pastry or graham-cracker crust.

Mix the cornstarch, sugar and salt.

Put the cottage cheese and sour cream in a mixer bowl and beat till smooth.

Add the sugar mixture.

Beat the yolks and add.

Remove from the mixer.

Beat the egg whites stiff but not dry, and fold into the cheese mix.

Fill the pie pan and sprinkle lightly with cinnamon sugar.

Bake at 450° F. for 10 minutes, then at 350° for 45 minutes more.

EARLY AMERICAN SUGAR COOKIES
(Makes approximately 2 dozen cookies)

Preheat oven to 375° F.

½ cup butter
1 cup sugar
2 eggs, well beaten
½ teaspoon salt
2 teaspoons baking powder
1 teaspoon vanilla or lemon extract
1 tablespoon milk
1½ cups unbleached sifted white flour
   (about)

Cream the butter, add the sugar, eggs, milk, and 1 cup flour mixed and sifted with the baking powder and salt.

Add enough more sifted flour to make of the right consistency to roll out.

Chill, roll, sprinkle with sugar, cut and bake in a moderately hot oven (375° F.) for about 8 minutes.

SAND COOKIES
(Makes 18 cookies)

Preheat oven to 375° F.

¼ pound butter
1¼ cups unbleached sifted white flour
1½ teaspoons double-acting baking powder
⅓ cup granulated sugar
1 teaspoon vanilla

Melt the butter over low heat and continue cooking, stirring occasionally, until golden brown, or for about 7 to 8 minutes.

Remove from the fire and stir with a wooden spoon until cool.

Sift together the flour and baking powder.

Add to this the sugar and sift again.

When the butter is cool, add the flour and sugar to the butter, a heaping tablespoon at a time, and work into a smooth paste.

Flavor with the vanilla.

Form into 1-inch balls, using your fingers, pressing the mixture firmly together.

Place on a buttered cookie sheet, making 18 balls.

Bake in a 375° F. oven until lightly browned, or for about 18 minutes.

Remove from the oven and cool, before removing from the tin with a spatula.

EXTRA-SPECIAL COOKIES
(Makes 16 cookies)

Preheat oven to 350° F.

⅓ cup pecans, chopped very fine
¼ cup granulated sugar
2 cups sifted flour
½ cup confectioner's sugar
¼ teaspoon baking soda
¼ pound sweet butter
1 whole egg
1 egg yolk
grated rind of 1 lemon
1 teaspoon vanilla
¼ cup thick jam, apricot or strawberry

Butter 2 large cookie tins lightly.

Mix together in a shallow saucer the chopped pecans and the granulated sugar.

Sift some all-purpose flour and measure out 2 cups.

Add to the flour the confectioner's sugar and baking soda, and sift into a large bowl.

Cut the butter into the flour mixture.

Work the butter into the flour and sugar, using a large silver fork.

Beat together in a cup the yolk of 1 egg with the vanilla and lemon rind.

Add this gradually to the first mixture.

It should be crumbly.

Gather the whole into a ball.

Work it with your hands, squeezing the dough until it sticks together and is smooth and well blended.

In a separate saucer break the whole egg and beat it well with a fork.

Place the dough in the center of a lightly floured pastry cloth or board and roll out to about 3/16 inch thickness.

With a lightly floured 3-inch scallop-edged cookie cutter, stamp out 16 rounds.

It will be necessary to gather up the scraps and press them together and roll them out again in order to make the required number.

Place 8 of them on one of the buttered cookie sheets.

With a 1½-inch cutter, make holes in the centers of the other 8, and put the small rounds aside temporarily.

Now dip the 8 circles you have made, one side only, first into the beaten egg and then into the nuts and sugar.

Place them on the second buttered cookie sheet, nut side up.

Paint the plain ones, including the tiny rounds, with a thin coating of the remainder of the egg yolk.

Tuck the small ones between the big ones wherever you can, then place both pans in a 350° F. oven and bake until lightly browned and firm to the touch, or for 15 to 20 minutes.

The ones with sugar and nuts will cook slightly faster than the others, so watch carefully.

Remove the pans from the oven and almost immediately loosen the cookies, using a pancake turner.

Allow to cool.

When cool, spread the plain ones with a coating of thick jam, using about a heaping teaspoon for each cookie.

Top each with a nut-topped cookie circle.

These are very pretty, generous, life-sized cookies and extra-specially good.

OATMEAL COOKIES

(Makes 4 dozen cookies)

Preheat oven to 325° F.

> 2 eggs
> 1 cup sugar
> 1 cup melted butter
> 2 tablespoons molasses
> 1 teaspoon baking soda
> 1 teaspoon cinnamon
> 2 cups rolled oats
> 1 cup raisins
> 3 cups unbleached white flour
> ¼ cup hot water

Beat the eggs, add the other ingredients and mix well.
Drop on a buttered cookie sheet.
Press flat.
Bake in a slow oven (325° F.) for about 15 minutes.

CHOCOLATE COCONUT MACAROONS

(Makes 2½ dozen cookies)

Preheat oven to 325° F.

> 1 square unsweetened chocolate
> 1 4-ounce package sweet cooking chocolate
> 2 egg whites
> ½ cup granulated sugar
> pinch salt
> 2 3½-ounce cans flaked coconut
> 1 teaspoon vanilla

Melt together in the top of a small double boiler, over hot water, the unsweetened chocolate and sweet cooking chocolate.

Stir until smooth, remove from the heat and cool.

Beat the egg whites with a rotary beater until stiff.

Then beat in gradually the sugar.

Add the vanilla and salt, and beat 4 to 5 minutes until very stiff.

Add the cooled chocolate and continue beating until well mixed.

Fold in the flaked coconut.

Drop by teaspoonfuls onto well-buttered cookie sheets, making 2½ dozen.

Bake in a 325° F. oven until stiff on the outside but still a little soft on the inside, or for about 16 minutes.

Remove from the oven and shortly after loosen with a spatula.

Remove from the pan when cold.

OATMEAL MUFFINS
(Makes 12)

Preheat oven to 400° F.

1 cup cooked oatmeal
2 cups sifted flour
3 tablespoons sugar
4 teaspoons baking powder
¾ teaspoon salt
½ cup milk
2 beaten eggs
3 tablespoons melted butter

Thin out the oatmeal with the milk.

Add the sugar and beaten eggs.

Sift together the flour, salt and baking powder and add to the oatmeal, mixing well.

Add the melted butter and bake in buttered muffin tins for about 25 minutes in a hot oven.

BAKING-POWDER BISCUITS

(Makes 12 biscuits)

Preheat oven to 450° F.

2 cups sifted flour
2 teaspoons double-acting baking powder
1 teaspoon salt
1 teaspoon sugar
4 tablespoons butter (*2 ounces*)
¾ cup milk

Sift together the flour, baking powder, salt and sugar.

With fingertips rub in the butter until the flour looks like coarse meal.

Add the milk and mix well to a soft dough.

Flour a board lightly, dump out the dough, pat out gently to ¾ inch thick and cut out pieces with a round biscuit cutter or cut in 2-inch squares.

Place on a well-buttered cookie sheet and bake in a very hot oven (450° F.) for about 12 minutes, or until golden brown.

BASIC TWO-EGG CAKE

Preheat oven to 375° F.

¼ pound butter
1 cup sugar
2 eggs, beaten
½ cup milk
1¾ cups sifted cake flour
½ teaspoon salt
2 teaspoons double-acting baking powder
½ teaspoon vanilla

Butter thoroughly 2 9-inch layer-cake pans, sprinkle with flour and shake each pan until it is evenly covered with a thin film of flour. Dump off any excess flour.

With a wooden spoon cream the butter well and gradually add the sugar.

Mix until very light and fluffy.

Add the beaten eggs and mix well.

Sift together the flour, salt and baking powder and add alternately with the milk to the butter mixture.

Beat well but only enough to mix thoroughly.

Add the vanilla.

Divide the batter between the 2 pans and bake in a 375° F. oven for 25 to 30 minutes.

Turn out onto a wire-mesh cake cooler and turn over immediately so the cake cools with the top of the layer up.

If you use an electric mixer, follow the directions closely and do not overbeat.

SOFT CHOCOLATE FILLING FOR LAYER CAKE

2 squares unsweetened chocolate
1 cup milk
6 tablespoons sugar
2 tablespoons flour
¼ teaspoon salt
1 teaspoon butter
½ teaspoon vanilla

Add the chocolate to the milk and heat in the top of a double boiler over boiling water until the chocolate is melted.

Beat well with an egg beater.

Mix together the sugar, flour and salt.

Add to the milk mixture and cook until thick (about 3 minutes), stirring constantly.

Add the butter and vanilla and cool before using on the cake.

POUND CAKE

(Makes 2 cakes)

Preheat oven to 350° F.

1 pound butter
1 pound fine granulated sugar
1 pound sifted cake flour
10 eggs
¼ teaspoon salt
1 teaspoon vanilla
¼ teaspoon mace

Cream the butter until very light and creamy.

Add the sugar a little at a time, continuing to mix, until very light.

Beat the egg yolks until thick and lemon-colored.

Add to the butter and sugar, mixing well.

Add the vanilla and mace.

Add gradually the sifted cake flour and salt and mix until smooth.

Beat the egg whites till stiff but not dry and fold into the batter.

Pour into 2 loaf pans 9 by 4 by 3 inches, well buttered and lined with buttered white paper, filling ⅔ full.

Bake in a 350° F. oven about 1¼ hours until golden brown and slightly shrunken from the sides of the pan.

CUPCAKES

(Makes 1 dozen medium-size cupcakes)

Preheat oven to 375° F.

Use the Basic Two-Egg Cake mix (p.129) and fill buttered and floured muffin tins ⅔ full.

Bake in 375° F. oven for 20 to 25 minutes until brown and slightly shrunken from sides of the cups.

Turn out onto a wire-mesh cake cooler.

When cool, sprinkle with powdered sugar or cover with an icing.

GINGERBREAD
(Serves 6–8)

I have used this gingerbread recipe for thirty years, but I have no idea where it came from.

Preheat oven to 375° F.

> 1 cup molasses
> 1½ cups boiling water
> 1 teaspoon baking soda
> ½ cup (4 ounces) butter
> 1 cup sugar
> ½ teaspoon salt
> 1 teaspoon ginger
> 2 teaspoons cinnamon
> 1 egg
> 2½ cups sifted flour
> 1 tablespoon double-acting baking powder

Combine the molasses with the boiling water and soda.

Allow to cool and then add to the butter, which has been creamed with the sugar.

Add the salt, ginger and cinnamon.

Beat well, add the well-beaten egg and the flour, which has been sifted with the baking powder.

Have the batter very thin. If the batter is not very thin, add a little more milk so that it runs off the spoon and "ribbons." Pour into 2 well-greased pans (11 by 7 by 1½ inches) and bake in a moderately hot oven (375° F.) for about 20 minutes. Then reduce the heat to 300° F. and bake for 20 minutes more.

Baking the cake in this way gives a very crisp, candied crust with a light, delicate crumb. Milk may be substituted for water.

Serve with Applesauce.

PLAIN PASTRY
(For a 2-crust pie)

I make a plain pastry for my crust, using good lard and the all-purpose flour with which I also make bread. I use a 9-inch pie pan.

Preheat oven to 450° F.

2½ cups sifted flour
1 teaspoon salt
6 ounces lard
6 tablespoons ice water

First sift the flour onto a piece of paper.

Then measure 2½ level cups of the sifted flour into a bowl.

Add the salt to the flour and stir well.

Cut the lard into small pieces, and as you cut, let them drop into the bowl.

Mix the lard into the flour with 2 knives or a pastry mixer until evenly distributed in very small bits.

Add the water bit by bit, stirring each moistened part with a fork.

This will seem very dry, but after all the water has been stirred in, press the dough together with your hands into a ball.

Wrap in waxed paper and chill while preparing your filling.

Roll out the pastry on a sheet of waxed paper lightly dusted with flour.

There are several gadgets available to help shape the pastry. I use a round wire circle, and I place half my dough in the center of it and roll out quickly in each direction to fill out the circle.

The bottom crust should be slightly larger than the top crust and should fit in the pan loosely. Trim off the edges, leaving about ½ inch to come up over the edge of the top crust.

Brush the inside of the bottom crust with egg white.

Fill carefully.

Roll out the top crust and fit it over the filling.

Fold up the edge of the lower crust and seal all around by pressing with your fingers.

Prick the top crust in several places.

Brush with beaten egg yolk or milk and bake in a very hot oven (450° F.) for 15 minutes, then reduce heat to 350° to finish baking, the time depending upon the filling.

PLAIN PASTRY WITH BUTTER
(For a 2-crust pie)

2½ cups sifted all-purpose flour
1 teaspoon salt
6 tablespoons vegetable shortening
6 tablespoons (¾ bar) sweet butter
6 tablespoons ice water

Sift together the flour and the salt.

Add the vegetable shortening and butter.

Work the shortening into the flour lightly, using your fingertips.

When mealy in consistency, moisten with 6 tablespoons ice water.

Form into 2 flat balls, wrap in waxed paper and chill until ready to use.

GRAHAM CRACKER CRUST

Preheat oven to 375° F.

1½ cups rolled graham crackers
¼ cup confectioner's sugar
6 tablespoons melted butter
¼ teaspoon powdered cinnamon

Put sufficient graham crackers through the meat grinder, using the medium blade, to give 1½ cups.

Add to these crumbs the confectioner's sugar sifted with the cinnamon.

Stir in the melted butter.

Pat the mixture firmly on the bottom and around the sides of a buttered 9-inch pie pan.

Bake in a 375° F. oven for about 15 minutes.

Cool before filling.

APPLE PIE

Preheat oven to 450° F.

Mix 1 recipe of Plain Pastry (p. 133).

6 to 8 tart apples, preferably Greening,
Baldwin or Northern Spy
1 tablespoon flour
¾ cup sugar
¼ teaspoon nutmeg
¼ teaspoon salt
1 tablespoon butter
grated rind of ½ lemon

Roll out the pastry for the bottom crust and line a 9-inch pie pan.

Brush with egg white.

Peel and slice the apples into a bowl.

Mix together the sugar, flour, nutmeg and salt, pour over the apples and toss well together.

Place the sugared apples in the pastry, dot with butter and lemon rind.

Wet the edge of the pastry.

Roll out the top crust and place over the apples.

Press the edges together.

Prick in several places and brush with beaten egg or milk so it will brown nicely.

Bake in a 450° F. oven for 15 minutes, then reduce heat to 350° and bake for 45 minutes more.

RHUBARB PIE

Preheat oven to 450° F.

Mix 1 recipe of Plain Pastry (p. 133).

> 2 cups rhubarb
> ¾ cup sugar
> 3 tablespoons flour
> dash nutmeg

Line a 9-inch pie pan with pastry.

Peel and cut the rhubarb into small pieces.

Mix the sugar, flour and nutmeg together.

Mix the rhubarb with the sugar mix and place in the pie pan.

Cover with a pastry top.

Prick the top with a fork and brush with beaten egg or milk.

Bake in a hot oven (450° F.) for 15 minutes.

Reduce heat to 350° and bake 45 minutes more.

Serve warm with thick cream to pour over it.

BLUEBERRY PIE

Preheat oven to 450° F.

Mix 1 recipe of Plain Pastry (p. 133).

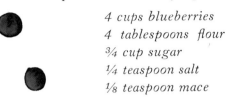

4 cups blueberries
4 tablespoons flour
¾ cup sugar
¼ teaspoon salt
⅛ teaspoon mace

Line a 9-inch pie plate with pastry.

Mix together the flour, sugar, salt and mace.

Sprinkle this mixture over the berries.

Cover with a pastry top.

Prick the top with a fork and brush with beaten egg or milk.

Bake in a 450° F. oven for 15 minutes.

Reduce heat to 350° and bake for 45 minutes more.

CUSTARD PIE

Preheat oven to 450° F.

Mix ½ recipe of Plain Pastry (p. 133).

4 eggs
¼ cup sugar
¼ teaspoon salt
2 cups milk
1 cup cream
nutmeg

Line a 9-inch pie pan with pastry.

Brush the inside with white of egg.

Chill.

Beat the eggs slightly with a fork, add the sugar and salt and stir till blended.

Add the milk and cream and blend well.

Place the pie pan on the oven shelf and gently pour in the custard.

Sprinkle a slight amount of nutmeg on the top.

Bake at 450° F. for 10 minutes, then reduce heat to 300° and bake for 50 minutes more, or until firm when tested with a knife.

COCONUT CUSTARD PIE

Use the recipe for Custard Pie (above).

Add ½ cup moist grated coconut to the egg mixture. Sprinkle the top with more coconut.

DEEP-DISH BLUEBERRY PIE

This is a great favorite and we have it often during the blueberry season because all we have to do is go out and pick our own berries.

Preheat oven to 400° F.
Mix ½ recipe for Plain Pastry (p. 133).

> *1 quart fresh blueberries*
> *½ cup sugar*
> *2 tablespoons flour*
> *¼ teaspoon salt*
> *½ teaspoon nutmeg*
> *2 tablespoons lemon juice*
> *1 tablespoon butter*

Wash the blueberries in cool water and pick over if necessary. Drain.

Mix together the sugar, flour, salt, nutmeg and lemon juice, and add to the blueberries, mixing very gently until the fruit is coated.

Turn into a deep 6-cup baking dish; dot with butter.

Cover with pie crust and bake in a hot oven (400° F.) for about 30 minutes until the crust is golden brown.

This is delicious either warm or chilled.

PRUNE OR APRICOT PIE

Preheat oven to 450° F.

Mix ½ recipe of Plain Pastry with Butter (p. 134).

> *¾ cup cooked sweetened prunes or apricot purée*
> *½ teaspoon grated lemon rind*
> *1 tablespoon strained lemon juice*
> *½ cup granulated sugar*
> *3 egg whites*
> *⅛ teaspoon salt*
> *1 cup slightly whipped cream*

Line a 9-inch pie plate with pastry.

Crimp the rolled-under edges prettily.

Prick with a fork and bake for about 15 minutes, or until lightly browned.

Cool and fill with the following mixture:

Rub cooked sweetened dried apricots or prunes through a sieve.

To ¾ cup of the purée, add ½ teaspoon grated lemon rind and 1 tablespoon strained lemon juice.

Add ⅛ teaspoon salt to 3 egg whites and beat until stiff, then beat in gradually ½ cup granulated sugar.

Fold this into the fruit purée and fill the cooked tart shell.

Reduce the heat of the oven to 325° F. and bake for about 20 minutes.

Serve soon after baking, while still warm, accompanied by a bowl of slightly beaten heavy cream.

RICH APPLE AND ALMOND PIE
(Serves 6–8)

Preheat oven to 400° F.

5 large apples
1 cup butter (2 bars)
1 cup sifted flour
1 cup blanched almonds, finely grated
1¾ cups granulated sugar
I cup heavy cream, whipped

For the pastry, cream the butter with 1 cup granulated sugar and beat until very light, then add gradually the sifted flour and almonds.

When well blended, shape into 2 balls, one slightly larger than the other.

Wrap in waxed paper, flatten a bit and chill until firm.

In the meantime, peel, quarter and core the apples.

Slice fine into a bowl, sprinkling with ¾ cup granulated sugar as you go along.

Now, working quickly, roll out on a floured pastry cloth the larger ball of pastry, making it about 12 inches in diameter.

Roll it up onto your rolling pin and unroll over a 10-inch pie plate.

Place immediately in the refrigerator for 5 minutes to prevent softening, then fill with the prepared apples.

Refrigerate again while you quickly roll out the smaller ball of pastry, making it just large enough to cover the apple-filled crust.

Roll up on the pin, working quickly, and unroll over the apples.

Press the edges together and crimp prettily.

Prick with a fork, place immediately in a 400° F. oven and bake for 15 minutes.

Reduce heat to 350° F. and continue cooking until the juices flow, or for about 1 hour in all.

Serve hot with plenty of whipped cream.

CHEDDAR CHEESE PIE
(Serves 4)

Preheat oven to 350° F.

> *slices of white bread*
> *butter*
> *½ pound sharp Cheddar cheese*
> *2 eggs*
> *1 cup milk*

Butter a 9- or 10-inch pyrex pie pan generously.

Butter enough slices of white bread, crusts removed, to line the pan's bottom and sides, buttered side down, cutting the bread to fit and overlapping here and there if necessary.

Slice the cheese into small pieces and lay evenly over the bread in the pie pan.

Beat the eggs in a small bowl.

Add the milk and pour over the cheese.

Bake at 350° F. about ½ hour until bubbly and golden brown.

Serve hot.

CARROT CHEESE PIE
(Serves 4)

Preheat oven to 350° F.

> *bread slices, buttered, crusts trimmed off*
> *4 ounces grated carrots*
> *4 ounces grated Cheddar cheese*
> *2 eggs*
> *1 cup milk*

Butter generously a 9- or 10-inch pyrex pie pan.

Line the pan with the slices of bread, buttered side down, cutting to fit the bottom and sides.

Put the grated cheese and carrots on top of the bread.

Beat the eggs with the milk.

Pour over the cheese mixture.

Bake in a moderate (350° F.) oven for 30 minutes.

TOMATO CHEESE PIE

(Serves 4)

Preheat oven to 350° F.

bread slices, buttered, crusts trimmed off
4 tablespoons dry bread crumbs
canned tomatoes
1 tablespoon grated onion
salt and pepper
1 teaspoon sugar
4 ounces grated Cheddar cheese
2 eggs
1 cup milk
1 extra egg white, slightly beaten

Butter generously a 9-inch pyrex pie pan.

Line the pan with the bread, buttered side down, cutting strips to fit around the sides.

Brush the bread surfaces with beaten egg white and sprinkle with the dry crumbs.

Drain the tomatoes from their juice and lay the tomatoes on the crumbs. Reserve the juice for other use.

Sprinkle with the salt, pepper, sugar and grated onion.

Add the grated cheese all over evenly.

Beat the eggs and milk together and pour over the cheese.

Bake for ½ hour at 350° F.

HOT APPLE TARTS

(Makes 6 tarts)

Preheat oven to 350° F.

6 baked patty shells
2 cups sliced tart apples
1 teaspoon lemon juice
1 cup apple juice or water
2 tablespoons water
¼ teaspoon cinnamon
⅔ cup sugar
pinch salt
3 tablespoons cornstarch
⅛ teaspoon nutmeg
¼ teaspoon lemon rind

Combine the apples, sugar, lemon juice, salt and apple juice or water.

Bring to a boil and simmer until the apples are tender.

Soften the cornstarch in 2 tablespoons water and stir into the juice.

Cook, stirring, until the juice is clear and thickened.

Stir in the spices and lemon rind.

Fill the baked shells; replace the caps.

Place on a baking sheet and sprinkle with sugar.

Bake in a 350° F. oven for 15 minutes.

Serve hot or warm with whipped cream.

INDEX

Almond Pie, Rich Apple and, 140

Ambrosia Rolls, 87–8

Apple

  Cake, 70–1

    Crisp, 73

    Crumb Coffee, 80–1

    Dutch, 77

    Orchard Delight, 62–3

  Danish, 102–3

  Kuchen, Fresh, 68–9

  Loaf, Cinnamon, 78–9

  Pie, 135–6

    Rich, and Almond, 140

  Tarts, Hot, 143

Apricot

  Peanut Squares, 88–9

  Pie, 139

Baking-Powder Biscuits, 128–9

Barmbrack, 114–5

Basic Sweet Dough—No Knead, 61

Basic Two-Egg Cake, 129–30

Basic Whole Meal Irish Soda Bread, 111

Batter Bread, White, 44

Biscuits, Baking-Powder, 128–9

Blueberry

  Pie, 137

    Deep-Dish, 138

Bread

  Barmbrack, 114–5

  Buttermilk, 50–1

  Corn, 51

  General Instructions for Making, 37–40

  Griddle, 113

  Hungarian Christmas, 54–5

  Maggie Murphy's Pot Oven, 111–2

  Potato Loaves, Old Fashioned, 56–7

  Soda, Basic Whole-Meal Irish, 111

    Raisin, 113

    White, 112

  Souper-Dooper, 58

  Wheat-Germ, 52–3

  White, 43

    Casserole, 49

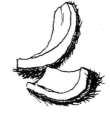

Quick Method, 47
Salt-Free, 48
Sponge Method, 45
Standard, 46
Whole-Wheat, Importance of, 36–7
Bread Sticks, Herb, 93
Brioche, 105–6
Brown-Sugar Frosting, 120
Buns
    Chocolate Sticky, 108–9
    English Bath, 92
    Saffron, 95–6
    Sally Lunn, 57
Buttermilk Bread, 50–1

Cake
    Basic Two-Egg, 129–30
    Cheese, 122
    Chocolate Icebox, 119
        Layer, 118
    Coconut Layer, 118
    Devil's Food, 117
    Gato-Almond, 121
    General Instructions, 115
    Layer, Soft Chocolate Filling for, 130
    Pound, 130–1
    Two-Layer, 116
Cake, Coffee
    Apple, 70–1
        Crisp, 73
        Crumb, 80–1
        Danish, 102–3
        Dutch, 77

Kuchen, Fresh, 68–9
    Loaf, Cinnamon, 78–9
    Orchard Delight, 62–3
Apricot Peanut Squares, 88–9
Chocolate Yeast, 72
Cinnamon Apple Loaf, 78–9
Coconut, 60
Danish Apple, 102–3
Dutch Apple, 77
Fruit (Double Choice), 64–5
Golden Twist Rings, 83–4
Lace, 74–5
Orange Loaf, 64
Peach Kuchen, Fresh, 66–7
Peanut Twist, 84–5
Quick 'N' Easy, 76
Swedish Cardamom Braid, 82–3
Cake, Frosting
    Brown-Sugar, 120
    Chocolate, 117–8
    Cream Cheese, 120
    Seven-Minute, Coconut, 118
    Vanilla, 120
Cake, Icing, Confectioner's Sugar, 63
Cardamom Braid, Swedish, 82–3
Carrot Cheese Pie, 141–2
Casserole White Bread, 49
Celery Crescents, Quick, 106–7
Cheddar Cheese Pie, 141
Cheese
    Cake, 122
    Crescents, 104
    Pie, Carrot, 141–2
        Cheddar, 141
        Tomato, 142

Chocolate
    Cake, Icebox, 119
        Layer, 118
        Yeast, 72
    Coconut Macaroons, 126–7
    Frosting, Old Fashioned, 117–8
    Soft Filling for Layer Cake, 130
    Sticky Buns, 108–9
Christmas Bread, Hungarian, 54–5
Cinnamon
    Apple Loaf, 78–9
    Crescents, 83–5
Coconut
    Cake, Layer, 118
    Coffee Cake, 60
    Custard Pie, 138
    Frosting, Seven-Minute, 118
    Macaroons, Chocolate, 126–7
Coffee Cake
    Apple, 70–1
        Crisp, 73
        Crumb, 80–1
        Danish, 102–3
        Dutch, 77
        Kuchen, Fresh, 68–9
        Loaf Cinnamon, 78–9
        Orchard Delight, 62–3
    Apricot Peanut Squares, 88–9
    Chocolate Yeast, 126–7
    Cinnamon Apple Loaf, 78–9
    Coconut, 60
    Danish Apple, 102–3
    Dutch, 77
    Fruit (Double Choice), 64–5
    Golden Twist Rings, 83–4

    Lace, 74–5
    Orange Loaf, 64
    Peach Kuchen, Fresh, 66–7
    Peanut Twist, 84–5
    Quick 'N' Easy, 76
    Swedish Cardamom Braid, 82–3
Confectioner's Sugar Icing, 63
Cookies
    Chocolate Coconut Macaroons,
    126–7
    Extra Special, 124–5
    Oatmeal, 126
    Sand, 123
    Sugar, Early American, 122–3
Corn
    Bread, 51
    Rolls, Raised, 99
Cream Cheese Frosting, 120
Crescents
    Celery, Quick, 106–7
    Cheese, 104
    Cinnamon (Rolls), 83–5
Crust, Graham Cracker, 135
Cupcakes, 131
Custard Pie, 137

Danish, Apple, 102–3
Deep-Dish Blueberry Pie, 138
Devil's-Food Cake, 117
Double Choice Cakes, 64–5
Dough
    Sweet, Basic, No Knead, 61
    Quick-Rising, 59
Dutch Apple Cake, 77

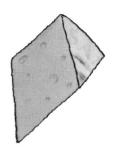

Early American Sugar Cookies,
    122–3
Easy Refrigerator Rolls, 91
English Bath Buns, 92
English Muffins, Whole-Wheat,
    see Refrigerator
    Whole-Wheat Rolls, 96–8
Extra-Special Cookies, 124–5

Figure 8's *see* Refrigerator Whole-
    Wheat Rolls, 96–8
Filling, Soft Chocolate, for Layer
    Cake, 130
Fresh Apple Kuchen, 68–9
Fresh Peach Kuchen, 66–7
Frosting, Cake
    Brown Sugar, 120
    Chocolate, Old Fashioned,
        117–8
    Cream Cheese, 120
    Seven-Minute, Coconut, 118
    Vanilla, 120
Fruit Cake, 65

Gato-Almond Cake, 121
Gingerbread, 132
Glaze, Sugar, 75
Golden Twist Rings, 83–4
Graham Cracker Crust, 135
Griddle Bread, 113

Herb Bread Sticks, 93

Hot Apple Tarts, 143
Hungarian Christmas Bread, 54–5

Icebox Cake, Chocolate, 119
Icing, Confectioner's Sugar, 63
Irish Soda Bread
    About, 110
    Basic Whole-Meal, 111

Kuchen
    Apple, Fresh, 68–9
    Peach, Fresh, 66–7

Lace Coffee Cake, 74–5
Light Rolls, 94

Macaroons, Chocolate Coconut,
    126–7
Maggie Murphy's Pot Oven Bread,
    111–2
Muffins
    Oatmeal, 128
    Whole-Wheat, English, *see*
    Refrigerator Whole-Wheat Rolls,
    96–8

Oatmeal
    Cookies, 126
    Muffins, 128
Old-Fashioned Chocolate Frosting,
    117–8

Old-Fashioned Potato Loaves, 56–7
Orange
    Glaze for Orange Loaf Cake, 65
    Loaf, 64

Pan-Fried Soda Bread, 113
Pan Ring, *see* Refrigerator Whole-
    Wheat Rolls, 96–8
Pastry
    Plain, 133–4
        with Butter, 134
Peach Kuchen, Fresh, 66–7
Peanut Squares, Apricot, 88–9
Peanut Twist, 83–5
Pie
    Almond, Rich Apple and, 140
    Apple, 135–6
    Apricot, 139
    Blueberry, 137
        Deep-Dish, 138
    Cheese
        Carrot, 141–2
        Cheddar, 141
        Tomato, 142
    Coconut Custard, 138
    Crust, Graham Cracker, 135
        Plain Pastry, 133–4
    Custard, 137
    Deep-Dish Blueberry, 138
    Prune, 139
    Rhubarb, 136
Plain Pastry, 133–4
    with Butter, 134
Potato Loaves, Old Fashioned, 56–7

Pot Oven Bread, Maggie Murphy's,
    111–2
Pound Cake, 130–1
Prune Pie, 139

Quick Celery Crescents, 106–7
Quick Method White Bread, 47
Quick 'N' Easy Coffee Cake, 76
Quick-Rising Sweet Dough, 59

Raised Corn Rolls, 99
Raisin, Soda Bread, 113
Refrigerator Rolls, Easy, 91
Refrigerator Whole-Wheat Rolls,
    96–8
Rhubarb Pie, 136
Rich Apple and Almond Pie, 140
Rich Golden Rolls, 100
Rolls
    Ambrosia, 87–8
    Brioche, 105–6
    Cheese Crescents, 104
    Chocolate Sticky Buns, 108–9
    Cinnamon Crescents, 83–5
    Corn, Raised, 99
    Easy Refrigerator, 91
    English Bath Buns, 92
    Figure 8's *see* Refrigerator
    Whole-Wheat Rolls, 96–8
    How to Shape, 86
    Light, 94
    Pan Ring, *see* Refrigerator
    Whole-Wheat Rolls, 96–8

Quick Celery Crescents, 106–7
Refrigerator Whole-Wheat, 96–8
Rich Golden, 100
Saffron Buns, 95–6
Shaped Batter, 90
Strip, *see* Refrigerator Whole-Wheat Rolls, 96–8
Sunday Breakfast, 101–2
Whole-Wheat English Muffins, *see* Refrigerator Whole-Wheat Rolls, 96–8

Saffron Buns, 95–6
Sally Lunn, 57
Salt-Free White Bread, 48
Sand Cookies, 123
Seven-Minute Coconut Frosting, 118
    Vanilla, 120
Shaped Batter Rolls, 90
Soda Bread
    About, 110
    Basic Whole-Meal, Irish, 111
    Griddle, 113
    Pan-Fried, 113
    Raisin, 113
    White, 112
Soft Chocolate Filling for Layer Cake, 130
Souper-Dooper Bread, 58
Sponge Method White Bread, 45
Standard White Bread, 46
Strip Rolls, *see* Refrigerator Whole-Wheat Rolls, 96–8

Sugar Cookies, Early American, 122–3
Sugar Glaze, 75
Sunday Breakfast Rolls, 101–2
Swedish Cardamom Braid, 82–3
Sweet Dough
    Basic, No Knead, 61
    Quick-Rising, 59

Tarts, Hot Apple, 143
Tomato Cheese Pie, 142
Two-Egg Cake, Basic, 129–30
Two-Layer Cake, 116

Vanilla, Seven-Minute Frosting, 120

Wheat-Germ Bread, 52–3
White Batter Bread, 44
White Bread, 43
    Casserole, 49
    Quick Method, 47
    Salt-Free, 48
    Soda, 112
    Sponge Method, 45
    Standard, 46
Whole-Meal Irish Soda Bread, Basic, 111
Whole-Wheat
    English Muffins, *see* Refrigerator Whole-Wheat Rolls, 96–8
    Rolls, Refrigerator, 96–8